Christian Heroines
Just Like You?

Christian
Heroines

Just Like You?

Catherine Mackenzie

CF4·K

10 9 8 7 6 5 4 3 2

© Copyright 2009 Catherine Mackenzie

ISBN: 978-1-84550-460-1

Reprinted 2014

Published by Christian Focus Publications,
Geanies House, Fearn, Tain, Ross-shire,
IV20 1TW, Scotland, U.K.
www.christianfocus.com
email:info@christianfocus.com

Cover design by Daniel van Straaten
Printed and bound in Denmark by Nørhaven

CONTENTS

JUST LIKE YOU AND ME?

Well – were they? Were these Christian women who span the centuries just like us? In what ways are we similar? In what ways do we differ? In what ways are they like Jesus Christ and how can we be more like him and them?

As you read the real life stories of these amazing people you will realise that they are indeed just like you. There are young teenagers, mothers, wives and single women. There are rich and poor, educated and uneducated. They are all heroines but they all have flaws – just like us. They are just ordinary girls and women who were given the gift of faith – faith in the one true God.

Some of these women show great bravery in the most dreadful circumstances. As we find out where their strength comes from, we will discover that this same strength is waiting for us to use in our lives.

God is the same yesterday, today and forever. It is his strength that these Christians relied on. He will be your strength too.

As we look at this list of women we come across something quite amazing about the Christian faith. Where else would you see noblewomen and slaves given the same honour and respect? Those who were born to privilege and those who were born in poverty are equal before the eyes of God. Even today the gospel of Christ still brings people from all backgrounds, religions and nationalities together.

During the years when Christianity was considered by many to be a new religion, those who followed Christ were forced to face hardships, struggles and even death for simply following the Lord Jesus Christ. In later years Christians faced execution for simply reading the Bible for themselves or standing up for the truth of God's Word.

These men, women and children are the martyrs of the Christian church. But there are others who didn't face the scaffold yet they suffered too. Many saw husbands killed or thrown in prison. Others gave their lives to serve Jesus in foreign lands and perished from disease. Some were turned out of house and home by unbelieving fathers or husbands. However, throughout the ages the blood of the martyrs has been the seed of the church. The lives and actions of believers have been used by God throughout history to spread his Word and build up his church. Many of these martyrs have been forgotten by the world, but in reading this book we endeavour to remember some of the women who are Christian heroines.

HOW THIS BOOK IS LAID OUT

There are different sections entitled:

THE EARLY CHURCH
THE REFORMATION
THE COVENANTERS
MODERN MISSIONARIES AND CHRISTIANS

Each of these sections begins with some ideas for *Things to do*. After each character's story there is a *Look It Up* section which will bring various Bible verses to light.

THE EARLY CHURCH

Women in this period of history were usually uneducated. Only some noble families educated their daughters. But the truth of the gospel of Jesus Christ touched the hearts of women from all backgrounds, when they were taught that there was one true God who would forgive their sins and love them equally with men. This was an amazing realisation. Many cultures at that time did not regard women as equals and even in a court of law their testimony was not seen to be as valid as a man's.

During the time of the Early Church the ruling power was the Roman Empire. This term was used to describe a territory which was under Roman rule.

Christian Heroines

Initially Rome was a Republic and it was during those days that the territory began to expand. The first emperor was Augustus and Roman power reached its peak under Emperor Trajan when it controlled over 5,900,000 square kilometres of land.

The persecuted Christians lived at various times throughout the empire's history. Different emperors organised varying degrees of persecution against the church.

Blandina suffered under Marcus Aurelius in the year 177; Perpetua and Felicity were martyred in the third century.

THINGS TO DO:

1. Go to a library and look out an atlas that has a map of the ancient Roman world.

- Find the capital city of Rome.
- Where is France and can you find the city of Lyons?
- Does this map show North Africa? If it does, look for the city of Carthage.

You will now have looked up all the places that feature in the next part of the book.

2. Go to a dictionary and look up the definition of martyr. Think about the different kinds of persecution that take place today. Are Christians persecuted in your country? How does this persecution compare to the Christians of the past and to Christians in other countries today?

BLANDINA
The Roman Slave Girl

Imagine you are a Roman slave. All day every day you must obey your master or mistress. You have no time to call your own and your owner can even sell you to another without as much as a by your leave. Even your children can be taken away from their family and home. It's not an easy thing to be a Roman slave, and it's even worse to be a Roman female slave. This was what Blandina was. There couldn't be anything worse, but in Roman times if you were also a Christian then life could be very hard indeed. However, Blandina might have argued that when she became a Christian she tasted freedom for the first time – real freedom that you can't get anywhere else.

The year was 177 and already the Church was beginning to tackle heresies and doctrinal errors while still coping with age old persecutions from its enemies. The good news of Jesus Christ was spreading. Wherever Christians went they brought with them the Word of God, the truth of salvation and a courage to stand up for what they believed in.

In the year 177, Lyons in France unleashed a savage persecution on believers. The persecution was so terrible that the philosopher Athenagoras risked his own life by writing to the then emperor, Marcus Aurelius, in order to plead for equal rights for Christians throughout his realm.

One of the persecuted Christians who inspired this courageous act was a young slave woman named Blandina. Let's find out a bit about the background to her life.

As a slave in Roman times, Blandina's life would not have been easy. She would have been the possession of her master or mistress to be bought and sold at will. Slaves often lead hard lives, suffering harsh punishments for any small mistake.

If there was anything worse than being a slave it was being a female slave. Blandina belonged to the lowest of the low in her society. But she was alive at a time when the good news of Jesus Christ was making headway across Europe. Christianity taught that all were one in Christ Jesus. It didn't matter if you were free or a slave, male or female, Greek or Jew – Jesus Christ, the Son of God was the Saviour of the world.

Anyone could come to him for forgiveness of their sins. Your skin colour didn't matter, your position in life was irrelevant – those who believed in Jesus Christ were all equal in God's eyes.

It must have been wonderful for a girl like Blandina to discover the truth of Jesus Christ for the first time. It's wonderful for anyone, but for Blandina it would have changed her life in so many ways. She was still a slave, but she knew the real truth. She knew that in Jesus Christ she was truly free and a child of God.

Now Christianity hadn't been in Lyons that long when the persecutions began. It had only been twenty-five years since Polycarp of Smyrna had sent Pothinus as a missionary to the area. A church had soon been established and as new believers flocked to its doors opposition to its teachings grew ever greater.

It started with Christians being banned from certain businesses. They weren't allowed to trade; a great hardship for those who were merchants and skilled workers. Christians were banned from certain houses, so life became more of a struggle than normal. Before long the persecutions escalated. Violent mobs roamed the streets looking for people to accuse as Christians.

Those who boldly confessed their faith in Christ would be beaten, stoned and robbed. If they happened to survive those tortures a prison cell awaited them. There they would remain until the governor visited the region. When he arrived they would be put on trial. This often involved beatings and torture. Any who survived that ordeal would be used as entertainment in the amphitheatre. The tortured Christians were cheaper than gladiators.

When Blandina was captured she and other Christians were herded together into the darkest dungeons in the prison and to make matters worse many underwent torture.

Blandina would have witnessed the painful death of Pothinus, the ninety-two-year-old bishop of Lyons who died as a result of the injuries he acquired during his burning. Another man, Sanctus stood firm in his faith despite the severe wounds he received at the hands of his enemies. The testimony of these two brave Christian men must have given strength and courage to Blandina as she faced her own time of trial.

From the depths of the prison cells below the amphitheatre the Christians would have heard the bloodthirsty cries of the mob as they yelled in anticipation at the entertainments to come.

In adjoining cells wild animals were whipped up to a frenzy by their handlers. The plan was that some of the Christians would be suspended from stakes in the hope that the animals would kill them more slowly.

Blandina was chosen for this treatment. She was hung from a post in the middle of the arena as the doors to the animal cages were unlocked. However, those who had planned the games were totally surprised at what happened next. None of the wild beasts paid any attention to Blandina. They didn't even touch her. The other Christians who witnessed this believed that it was God who had delivered her.

Blandina was eventually removed from the amphitheatre and returned to the prison cells. But on the last day of the games she was again brought into the arena. A young boy named Ponticus joined her. He was just fifteen years old. Even when they were forced to watch other Christians being tortured neither Ponticus or Blandina would deny their faith.

Ponticus died first. Then Blandina was enclosed in a net and thrown in the path of a wild bull. Even in the midst of her pain and suffering Blandina cried out, 'I am a Christian and there is nothing vile done by us.'

As her body was removed from the arena, even those who had been screaming for her death moments before, had to admit that they had never before seen such courage.

LOOK IT UP:

1. Go to a dictionary and look up the definition of the word 'courage'.

2. On the television news or in the newspaper can you find examples of people who have shown courage?

3. Look up the following verses in your Bible: Psalm 55:16, 22; 1 Peter 5:7. How might someone who read these verses feel courageous? What is it about these verses that would make you feel brave?

PERPETUA OF CARTHAGE
The Roman Noblewoman

I magine that you are a young woman not long married. You've just given birth to your first child and you'd do anything for your new baby to give it the best start in life. You belong to a wealthy family and you've had every advantage yourself – such as a good education, anything money can buy. But there has always been something missing in your life. When you hear about Jesus Christ for the first time, you realise that the one thing you have been searching for is not a thing, but a person – and that person is God! Perpetua discovered this and very shortly after that, she discovered that believing in Jesus Christ was a dangerous thing to do if you were a Roman.

Perpetua lived in the City of Carthage which was in the country of Tunisia in North Africa. After several wars with Rome, Carthage eventually came under Roman occupation and by the first century the city had been completely rebuilt. It eventually became one of the three most important cities of the Roman Empire.

The Roman empire at that time ruled over a large part of the then known world. You could in fact travel from Carthage in North Africa to the cold shores of Britannia in Northern Europe and still be under Roman rule. Being under Roman occupation was difficult if your country continued to rebel against their authority. However, if the natives were willing to submit to the Roman legions then things could go well for them. Rome was responsible for bringing many advances to the lands that it conquered.

Roads would be built, as well as theatres and other wonderful things. However, the Roman empire always brought with it Roman gods. Many Christians were thrown into prison because they refused to sacrifice to these gods. They believed in the teachings of the Old and New Testaments which taught that there was only one God – but that God had three persons – God the Father, God the Son and God the Holy Spirit. Christians trusted in Jesus Christ who was God the Son and who had been crucified by the Romans only to rise again three days later. This teaching was totally against the pagan culture that Rome followed.

Romans worshipped any god that they pleased – and even some gods that they didn't know

(Acts 17: 22-31). When Christians insisted on teaching that the one true God was in fact a man who had been killed on a cross, but had risen from the dead – the Romans were furious. The teachings of Jesus Christ were seen as a threat and therefore the Christians were to be feared and hated.

At the beginning of the second century in the year 203 the Roman Emperor Severus began a ruthless persecution of the Christians. Perpetua was caught up in the middle of. It was during that time that she was thrown in prison for her faith.

Prison at the beginning of the second century was a truly horrible experience. There would have been very little food. You would have to depend on relatives to bring you what little food they could spare. However, many who were thrown in prison never saw their families again.

This is what makes it amazing that so many Christians were willing to stand firm in their faith. They would have known how dreadful the prisons were. They would also have known that the Roman authorities would probably kill them if they refused to give up their faith in Christ. Yet many continued to worship their Lord and Saviour Jesus Christ – even within the prison walls or on the sand of the amphitheatre.

Young people were often killed along with their parents. Whole families would be killed in the arena. But Perpetua was different. She was young, just twenty-two years old, but she was the only Christian in her family and her father did all he could to make her change her mind. However, Perpetua had been given a good education which meant that as well as being fluent in Latin and Greek, she could also think for herself. She would not give in to her father's pleadings to denounce Jesus.

When she was thrown in prison, her ability to read and write also meant that she could keep a diary. So not only is Perpetua one of the first Christian martyrs – she is also one of the first female Christian writers.

As soon as Perpetua arrived in prison she was baptised- so she must have been a very new Christian. She was also sent to prison with her new born baby. Thankfully Perpetua's father still loved her despite her decision to become a Christian. He often visited her in prison in order to give her food or clothing. Perhaps he hoped that his kindness would persuade her to renounce Christianity. But Perpetua remained steadfast to Christ even when her father threatened her with violence.

During one of his visits Perpetua turned to him and said, 'Father, do you see this little pitcher lying on the ground? Can I call it by any other name than what it is?'

'No, my daughter, you cannot,' was his reply.

'So also,' she answered, 'I cannot say of myself that I am anything else but a Christian.'

This was the last straw for Perpetua's father who totally lost all control and flung himself at his daughter in a fit of rage. In Perpetua's own words, 'He threw himself on me, as if he would have torn out my eyes, but he only hurt me and then went away.'

Perpetua would not have another visit from her father for quite some time. Meanwhile she was thrown into a dark dungeon, and her baby son was taken from her. She must have been very anxious about her young child, but despite this she endured great physical pain and violence from the guards and other prisoners.

Eventually her child was returned and she soon regained the strength that she had lost. 'The prison became to me as a palace, and I preferred to be there rather than anywhere else.'

The day appointed for the trial soon arrived. Perpetua's father tried once again to persuade his daughter to renounce Christ. He urged her to take pity on her aging parents; her grieving mother and the soon to be motherless child. He continually reminded her that her actions put their whole family in danger. It was very likely that her decisions would destroy not only her life, but the life of her father, mother and infant child. 'If you should suffer, none of us will be able to open our mouths freely.'

With tears in her eyes, Perpetua's only answer was, 'God's will be done.'

The public trial which followed was brief. When she was brought forward, her father appeared with the baby in his arms. However much he appealed to his daughter nothing that he said had any effect.

The Consul in charge of the trial also attempted to influence her without success. Perpetua would not change or alter.

'I am a Christian. I sacrifice not to idols.'

She was sentenced to be torn to death by wild beasts.

According to Roman custom, the night before the execution a large public supper was given to those who were condemned to death. It was often a splendid and magnificent occasion, but Perpetua took no part in it. She chose instead to spend her time in prayer.

It must have been a frightening prospect for the young woman as she stood at the entrance to the amphitheatre. The jeering of the crowds would have been deafening as they waited, excitedly, for her death. But Perpetua is reported to have left the prison and entered the arena with a gladness and a peace singing hymns of praise and joy.

Even as she lay dying after being wounded by a wild bull, she encouraged other Christians nearby, exhorting them to 'Continue firm in the faith, love one another, and be not moved because of my sufferings.' Perpetua was finally killed by a sword.

LOOK IT UP

1. Loyalty – look up a dictionary to find the definition of the word 'loyalty'.

2. Can you think of different ways in which you can see loyalty at work in day to day life? Can you see it in your own family or town?

3. Look up Psalm 40: 9-11. The word faithful is similar to loyal. Who is being loyal in these verses – is it the one who is writing the Psalm or is it the one he is writing the Psalm for?

FELICITY
A Young Mother

What would it be like to be thrown in prison when you are only a few weeks away from giving birth? You are a slave and have been captured along with your Christian owner. However, you also love Christ and are glad to be with God's people in their suffering. You are frightened as you face the prospect of death – but you know that God will give you courage.

This is what happened to Felicity. She must have worried about her baby, but she trusted her Lord in all things. Perhaps she wondered what it would be like to live in a world where you were free to live and worship; a world of freedom for her child.

Felicity's story is similar to Perpetua's as they were both in prison at the same time. The major difference is their backgrounds. Felicty was Perpetua's slave.

It was not uncommon for the slaves of the nobility to accompany them into prison, but Felicity was put in prison because she also was a believer in Jesus Christ.

At the time of their imprisonment Felicity was heavily pregnant. As the time drew closer for their execution Felicty was worried that she would not be permitted to die with the others. It was against Roman law to kill any woman who was with child.

However, two days before the games began Felicity gave birth to a little girl. The child was taken away and adopted by another Christian woman. On the appointed day Felicity was sent with the others to the arena.

At the demand of the mob the Christians were at first scourged, then attacked by wild boars, bears, leopards and men. Finally the women were wounded by wild animals before they were killed by the sword.

It has been noted that if you put the names of Perpetua and Felicity together and translate them into English you have the phrase Eternal Peace.

It is a beautiful thought when you think about what these two women went through. And it is a beautiful thought for those of us who trust in the Lord Jesus Christ, the Prince of Peace, that there is an eternal peace waiting for all those who belong to him.

LOOK IT UP

1. If the word 'felicity' means peace, what exactly does the word peace mean? Look it up in a dictionary.

2. Have you heard about peace talks in the news? What takes place during those events? Why is peace such an important thing?

3. Look up Psalm 119: 165. What kind of peace is being talked about here? Is it the same as the peace that politicians look for or is it different?

THE REFORMATION

When we hear of the Reformation we hear names of men like Luther and Calvin – the Fathers of the Reformation. But if you wish to find the mothers of the Reformation look beyond the pulpit to the martyr's pyre. That is where women take their place firmly beside the men.

Again we see the miracle of God at work through all social classes. Young girls who were married into the nobility stand beside elderly housewives, proclaiming Christ. We see God given courage light up their lives. Women, who are often referred to as the weaker sex, radiate strength and power when filled with the Holy Spirit and God's truth.

The Reformation was a movement that resulted from the need to reform the Roman Catholic Church. The leadership of Popes and Cardinals had lost sight of the truth of God's Word. Superstition and greed had crept into the worship. Those who should have cared for the people were now robbing them blind. Indulgences were purchased by the ignorant populace in the hope that these scraps of paper would bring them eternal life.

At the same time the church forbad the people from reading God's Word for themselves for in those pages they would have found out the truth that salvation is free and that the good works of human beings can do nothing to purchase forgiveness of sins.

THINGS TO DO

1. Start your own time line by taking a large sheet of paper. Draw a line from one end of the paper to the other. Find the earliest date in the book and write that at one end and then put this year at the other end. Every time a date is mentioned in the book slot it into the time line with a brief description.

2. Find a dictionary and look up the word 'reform' – what does it mean?

3. If you have access to the internet look up the names of Martin Luther and John Calvin. Their names are often mentioned when people discuss the Reformation. Can you find out what countries they came from and the names of the women they married? If you don't have access to the internet look up this information in a library.

ANNE ASKEW
Forced into marriage

What was it like to be a young noble girl living during the reign of King Henry VIII? Your family has ambitions. You don't care for those ambitions yourself – you'd prefer to be left with your books, your prayers and your dreams. But nobody listens to you. You're just a girl – someone to be married off to a rich landowner. This is what life was like for Anne Askew. When Anne's sister suddenly died her family decided that the best thing they could do was to marry Anne off to her sister's rich fiancée. What would life be like for a young Christian girl, forced to marry an ungodly man who detested even the idea of Bible reading? Anne Askew's story will tell you.

King Henry VIII of England was infamous for how he treated his enemies and mistreated his wives. He had six wives, two of whom were beheaded for adultery. But there were many ordinary people who faced the executioner simply because they either disagreed with the King or would not follow his commands concerning religious matters.

During that time of history it was the general rule that crimes such as murder were punishable by death. Other serious crimes would be punished in other ways such as by having a hand cut off or by being whipped. One of the methods of execution was burning. The prisoner would be taken from the cell to the stake – a large post erected in the middle of a mound of wood and other flammable materials. The accused would be tied securely to the post and the surrounding wood set alight. They were then left to burn to death.

Henry authorised many executions, but one of the last martyrs that he ordered to be burned at the stake was Anne Askew. She was killed on 25 July 1546 at twenty-five years of age.

As the second daughter of Sir William Askew of Kelsey in Lincolnshire Anne belonged to a family with great wealth and good connections. Anne's father was a prominent landowner who served in the royal court.

After the death of her mother, Anne had been raised by her father and step-mother and though it was unusual for girls to be educated in those days Anne received a good education at home.

With all the advantages she had had in life – a prosperous marriage was not only expected of her – it was her duty.

Marriages in those days were arranged by parents in the same way that we make business partnerships today. Often noble families chose future husbands or wives simply on the basis of how much money could be earned. Young women would often be given money as a dowry to give to their new husband and his family. A rich husband for a young daughter would often bring trade and other advantages to the girl's family.

A great marriage to a wealthy landowner was what had been planned for Anne's sister, Martha. Thomas Kyme was a neighbour of the Askew family and considered to be an excellent choice of husband. He was a Roman Catholic and very wealthy. However, Martha died before the marriage could take place. This was a disaster for Mr and Mrs Askew as they would now lose out on the wealth and privileges Thomas Kyme would have brought to their family.

A plan was instantly hatched to offer Anne in marriage to Thomas Kyme instead. Thomas was well known for being an unpleasant, foolish and ungodly character. Whereas Anne was an educated young girl who loved to study her Bible. It must have been obvious to her parents that this match would not be a happy one. However, Anne was forced to marry Kyme. It was her parents dearest wish. Anne's wishes would not have been considered even if she had had the courage to speak out against the arrangement.

During this marriage she repeatedly turned to her Bible for comfort. In those days it was rare to see people reading the Bible for themselves. The church did not approve of it and priests called it heresy. Thomas did all he could to force Anne to stop.

However, none of his arguments or threats had any effect on her whatsoever. She would not give up reading God's Word.

Eventually Anne became a mother. Shortly after the birth of her second child, Thomas Kyme issued the threat that if she continued to read her Bible he would throw her out of his house. Anne replied that she could not, and would not stop reading God's Word – it was her duty to read. It was a great comfort to her. Thomas could rant and rage all he liked – nothing he said could change her mind. So Anne and her two children were banished.

Anne had to return to her parents home. The situation became so bad that she even changed her name back to Askew. However, despite this action her husband and his family continued to harass her so Anne considered a move to the city of London. As she thought on it more and more – she realised that this indeed was the right thing for her to do. For many months now she had longed to be able to share the good news of Jesus Christ with others. At least in London she might be able to speak her mind and share the gospel with others. Nobody knew her there – and it would certainly be easier to hide from prying eyes in such a big metropolis.

However, even the big city was no refuge for Anne as her husband told the authorities what his wife was planning and spies were sent to follow her. News of her movements were then reported back to the Bishop of London, and to the Lord Mayor.

Anne knew the risks, but she still spoke out against the false doctrines of the church and distributed Protestant books which had been banned. It wasn't long before she was arrested and summoned before a tribunal to be questioned about her beliefs.

One of the doctrines that she refused to agree with was the doctrine of Transubstantiation which was a doctrine followed by the Roman Catholic church as well as the Church of England at that time. Those who held to that belief declared that the bread and wine served at the Lord's Supper were actually changed into the body and blood of the Lord Jesus Christ. They believed that when the bread was eaten it became Christ's flesh and that when the wine was drunk it became Christ's blood. Roman Catholics called this the Mass. Protestants did not take part in the mass and Anne Askew regularly spoke out against it.

A judge at the tribunal accused her of preferring to read five lines in the Bible than attend five masses. Anne admitted that this was true because reading God's Word did much to strengthen her while attending mass did nothing at all.

Finally she was asked if she believed that it was helpful to say masses for the souls of those who had died. Anne declared that it was a great idolatry to rely on saying mass as the only way to obtain eternal life was through the death of Christ.

Anne was then placed under guard and a priest was sent to give her advice. When asked later if he gave her good advice Anne simply replied, 'He did not!'

Further questioning by the Bishop of London amounted to nothing and then Anne was ordered back to prison. Thankfully she still had friends in the city and some of them were men and women with influence. It wasn't long before they arranged for her to be released from prison on bail.

This time of freedom would last just twelve months. But during this time important changes were taking place in the country. One of which was the conduct of King Henry's new queen, Catherine Parr. She was greatly in favour of the Protestant Revolution, and did what she could to help the spread of the gospel.

The priests and bishops began to get nervous. If the Queen was for the Protestants then they might be in danger themselves. Plots were hatched against Queen Catherine until they decided that it might be easier to attack her friends. If one of the Queen's associates could be forced into accusing her of treason they would then be able to condemn the Queen to death. It just so happened that Anne Askew was one of Catherine Parr's close friends and supporters. They arrested her yet again and imprisoned her in Newgate.

The accusers were determined to cast slurs on her character and when one of them asked her why it was that she had been separated from her husband, they were sure that this would show her up as an unfaithful woman. However, Anne simply stated that all the information regarding that part of her life was already known to the court. If they wished her to tell it one more time then she would tell it to the king and to the king alone.

'Do you think that the king has time to be troubled with the likes of you?' laughed the Lord Mayor.

'Why not?' Anne replied. 'Solomon was the wisest king that ever lived, yet he had the time to hear two poor common women. Why should my king not hear his simple, faithful subject?'

The trial continued with question after question and answer after answer. They asked her again about the bread and wine used at the Lord's Supper. Several members of the court urged her to change her beliefs, but she would not.

At the end of the trial she was once again returned to prison. However, when she was there Anne fell seriously ill. Her captors gave no thought towards her recovery. It wasn't long before she was once again placed on trial.

By Anne's own account we learn what happened next. 'They said to me that I was a heretic, and condemned by the law, if I would stand in my opinion. I answered that I was no heretic, neither did I deserve death by the law of God. But as concerning the faith which I uttered, I would not deny it, because I knew it to be true...After that they willed me to have a priest; and then I smiled. Then they asked me if it were not good. I said I would confess my faults unto God, for I was sure that He would hear me with favour.' After that the judges sentenced Anne Askew to be thrown into the dungeons and tortured. Her captors hoped that this would force her to let slip the names of other Protestants – possibly even the Queen. However, Anne remained resolute. Not one name passed her lips except for the name of God as she quietly prayed throughout the whole ordeal.

Even when they told her that she must be burned at the stake she remained calm. 'I would rather die than break with my faith,' was her reply.

In the days before her execution Anne was in so much pain that she could not stand. However, those friends who were allowed to visit her reported that despite her severe discomfort, Anne was at peace and her face was smiling throughout.

Executions in those days took place at Smithfield – a large open place close to the city of London. When she was tied to the stake there, the Lord Chancellor assured her of the King's pardon if she would recant. 'I came not hither to deny my Lord,' she answered. Word was then given to light the fire and very soon it all was over.

LOOK IT UP

1. Go to a dictionary and look up the definition of the word 'faith'. What does this mean?

2. What sort of person is someone who has great faith? Are they always right? What if someone has great faith in something that is completely wrong? What would happen then?

3. Read Ephesians 3:12-17. What does faith help us to do? Is there more than one faith? Read Ephesians 4:5. Is faith something we chose or is it something we are given? Read Ephesians 2:8.

JOYCE LEWES
Fashion or Faith

Imagine that you are a young noble woman with very little to occupy your mind and daily activities other than to make sure you look your best. You have an active social calendar and many friends and associates to call on. Your wardrobe is extensive, your hats alone could be sold for a small fortune, but your conversation is limited to court gossip and future parties. The problems of the poor concern you very little – but you occasionally give some coins to a beggar. This was the life of the young Joyce Lewes before her eyes were opened and she saw her world for what it really was. A world where faith and truth could be a matter of life or death.

For those of you who are familiar with Queen Mary's reign it might surprise you that it was welcomed in 1553 with open arms by those following the reformed faith. She came to the throne with promises of freedom, but it wasn't long before the Spanish inquisition became a fact of life on English shores. Those who followed the Protestant faith were hunted down and often put to death.

However, for one young woman, Joyce Lewes, these religious feelings and current events meant precious little. History may have been taking place just outside her doorway – but her seamstress was also making her a new outfit. Would anything ever shake this young woman from her dreams of fabrics and fashions? Well, one day something did.

The young mistress just happened to overhear some idle gossip from her servants. Perhaps they didn't mean to talk about such things in front of her, but they did. When Joyce discovered that several people had been burned at the stake in Coventry she was completely taken aback.

'Whatever for?' was the young woman's instant reaction to the news.

One servant replied that they weren't quite sure what the problem was, but that they had been told it was something to do with the new Protestant religion.

For the first time in the whole of her life young Joyce focused on something other than her appearance. Burnings and martyrs were issues totally foreign to her young mind – but she was determined to find out why they had taken place in Coventry of all places. 'Perhaps I should discuss this with my husband?' she wondered. But on second thoughts she chose her neighbour, John Glover. He was intelligent and seemed to be very keen on religious matters. 'I'm sure he'll be able to explain things to me,' she said.

When Joyce came to call on her neighbour he could see that she was genuinely concerned so took the opportunity to share the gospel message with her. Though Joyce would have been brought up to attend the cathedral and listen to the priests she probably knew very little about the Bible or about the Lord Jesus Christ. When John Glover told her that she was a sinner and deserving of punishment from God – she felt truly convicted. For the first time in her life Joyce became ashamed about her vanity. Here she was, rich and well dressed, with more money than she knew what to do with – yet inside, in her soul she was rotten and full of sin. 'I am undeserving of the mercy of God – yet the Bible is so clear. God loved the world so much that He sent his one and only Son so that whoever believed in Him should not perish, but have everlasting life.'

Joyce realised that it wasn't priests or popes who gave salvation, it wasn't her prayers or good works – it was the blood that Christ shed on the cross that purchased forgiveness of sins and eternal life. The church had told her many lies in the past. Now Joyce knew the truth. You could not buy salvation with money, or with pilgrimages. You didn't need the priest to intercede when Jesus Christ your Saviour was all the intercession that you needed. Forgiveness of sins was obtained from God alone.

John Glover explained the real meaning of the Lord's Supper or Eucharist to Joyce. So when she realised that the bread and wine did not actually turn into the physical body and blood of Christ she knew exactly what she should do.

'So many of the Church's practices are against God's law,' she murmured to herself. 'From this day on,' she admonished herself, 'I am determined to follow God's Word and stop attending the mass.'

However, this resolution of Joyce's brought her to the attention of the Bishop who issued a summons for her to be brought before him. Mr Lewes was furious. Stomping his foot he turned on the messenger and waved the Bishop's summons in his face. 'He may be a Bishop and high up in the church, but this gives him no right to be so disrespectful of my wife. Take your master's insinuations away with you or I'll force this paper down your throat until you eat it – every last scrap of it!'

The messenger did not believe the threat so refused to comply. Lewes then grabbed the young man and by holding a dagger at his heart forced him to eat the message until there was not even a small corner left.

Coughing and spluttering the young man stared blankly at Mr Lewes, hardly believing what had just happened. However, Mr Lewes must have felt slightly guilty for his behaviour as he instructed a servant to bring the messenger a glass of water before he went on his way.

Mr Lewes probably thought that that would be the end of the matter. However, it wasn't long before both Joyce and her husband were summoned to appear before the Bishop.

Mr Lewes now began to realise the seriousness of the situation and begged the Bishop's forgiveness for treating his servant in such a fashion.

'I will pardon you on one condition,' the Bishop announced. Mr Lewes waited with baited breath to hear the Bishop's decree.

'That condition,' the Bishop continued 'is that your wife submits to attending services once more.'

Instead of letting her husband answer for her Joyce spoke for herself. 'Why should I submit, for I have done nothing wrong,' she declared. 'I have not offended God or any of his laws.'

The Bishop was furious, but could not punish her until she had had some time to change her mind. One hundred pounds bail money was paid to the Bishop by Joyce's husband who also had to promise to present his wife before the court in a month's time.

Joyce spent much of her time during the next few weeks in prayer. Other believing friends joined her while other friends and family urged her husband to find some way to save his wife.

'You don't have to take her back to the Bishop, do you?' someone asked.

'What!' Mr Lewes exclaimed. 'And forfeit my £100? I will forfeit nothing for her sake!'

So on the fourth week after the initial enquiry Mr Lewes gave his wife over to the Bishop paying little heed to the fact that he was certainly handing her over to her executioners. Joyce Lewes was of less value to her husband than £100. He had no care for the suffering that she would go through or for the fact that he would not see her alive again.

Captivity and questioning was now the daily routine for the young Joyce. Question after question was fired at her about why she would not attend the mass. The Bishop would not give up in his questioning. And Joyce would not give up her belief.

When quizzed yet again about why she refused to attend mass Joyce replied, 'I find not these things in God's Word, which you so urge and magnify as things most needful for men's salvation. If these things were in the same Word of God commended, I would with all my heart receive, esteem, and believe them.'

Joyce Lewes was then declared to be a heretic and a sentence was passed that she was to be burned at the stake. However, the sheriff refused to put her to death, and for a whole year she lay in prison. When the day for execution was finally announced Joyce asked her friends how she should die in a way that glorified God. 'As for the fear of death,' she said, 'that does not trouble me. When I behold the amiable countenance of Christ my Saviour, the ugly face of death has no influence over me.'

What a change had come over this young woman in the matter of just a couple of years. Gone was the vain, foolish child – and in her place stood a godly, committed Christian.

The evening before her execution two priests were sent to her cell. They wanted her to make confession to them. But Joyce knew that as a Christian she could go straight to God to confess her sins. It was only He who could forgive sins. Joyce told the priests that she had already made her confession to Christ, at whose hands she was sure of forgiveness for her sins. 'I have nothing to say to you.'

On the following morning the sheriff came to her cell, and said, 'Mistress Lewes, I am come to bring you tidings of the Queen's pleasure, the which is, that you shall live no longer than one hour in this world; therefore prepare yourself thereunto.'

'Master Sheriff,' she replied, 'your message is welcome to me, and I thank my God.'

That morning the streets were lined with people and a huge crowd was gathered around the stake to witness her death. As she prayed her last prayer to deliver her country from false religion she was tied with chains around her waist. When the fire was lit she didn't even struggle – and calmly waited to be received into heaven at last.

LOOK IT UP

1. In a dictionary look up the definition of the word 'truth'. What does it mean?

2. Turn on the television news or read a newspaper. Can you see examples of how society is effected by those who chose not to tell the truth? How important is truth in everyday life?

3. What does the Bible say is real truth? Read Psalm 119: 160.

JOANE WASTE
The Blind Woman who could See

Most of us who can see have tried to imagine what it would be like to be blind. We put out our hands in order to feel our way around. When you've been used to the light it's hard to go about in the dark. However, it would be next to impossible for those of us who can see to imagine what it would be like to never have seen anything at all. If you had been born blind many things would be different for you today. In the 1500s if you had been born blind life was very hard indeed.

Our next heroine had struggled with blindness from birth – yet as it turns out she had been given the precious gift of spiritual sight.

Joane Waste was the daughter of William Waste, a poor, but honest man who worked as a rope maker. The family came from the parish of Allhallows near, Derby. It would have been a sad time for the family when they realised that their little girl had been born blind. Young Joane's prospects in life were very dim indeed. However at the age of about twelve years old she learned to do some work with her hands and gradually became skilled enough to assist her father in the rope making business.

When her parents died Joane was not left destitute. She went to live with her brother, Roger Waste. It was at this time that we know she was attending church. King Edward VI was on the throne and as a strong Protestant monarch he was influential in reforming the English church. During his brief reign many people came to follow the Reformed faith. One of these was Joane. She loved to go to church and would go each day if she could. In the church it didn't matter that she was blind because there she heard God's Word being read in her own tongue – and not in the Latin language that she had no understanding of. Week after week Joane determined to set aside what little money she could afford in the hope that one day she would be able to purchase a New Testament of her own.

This was a huge undertaking and almost impossible for a poor blind woman in those days. But somehow or other a New Testament was provided for her. Because she could not read Joane had to persuade a local man, John Hurt, to read for her. Because this man was a prisoner in the local jail he had plenty of time on his hands and was quite willing to read for Joane when he was able. It was Joane's aim to memorise as much of scripture as she could so that she would be able to recite the scripture whenever she had need of it. When no one was available to read to her she would travel into town to find one of the professional readers. These were men who charged money to read a certain amount of words to the illiterate. So one way or another Joane Waste heard the Bible read aloud. And over time she learned to recite whole chapters of it.

Joane's church attendance not only taught her about the scripture, but it also made her aware of the many ways in which the Roman Catholic church had abused religion in the past. She was taught that there was only one way to get to heaven, which was through the death and resurrection of God's Son, the Lord Jesus Christ.

However, on the death of King Edward the situation in England changed. Freedom of religion vanished under the reign of his sister, Queen Mary. Her violent rule ensured that many abandoned the Protestant faith. Yet Joane, one poor blind woman, continued to read the Bible and worship just as she had done in King Edward's time.

When the Bishop heard of her rebellion he called Joane in to bear witness. The charges laid against her were as follows: She was guilty of declaring that the bread and wine were not the actual body and blood of Christ, but simply a representation.

Now the men who accused her tried to trip her up with all sorts of sophisticated arguments, but Joane showed great strength of conviction. She declared that all she believed was what the Holy Scriptures taught her. 'Do not trouble this poor blind woman any further with your talk,' she insisted. 'By God's assistance I am ready to yield up my life in whatever way you should appoint.'

Her accusers did not at first give in to her demands. They continued to threaten her and coax her in turn. She demanded that they should solemnly swear to the fact that their doctrine was true and that hers was false – and that they should also be willing to stand in her place on the Judgement day in order to attest to that fact before Almighty God. However, none of her accusers had the strength or the conviction to agree to that. They were willing to persecute a reformer, but they weren't willing to stand up for their own faith. Joane declared that she had nothing further to say except that she was willing now for them to do whatsoever they wished.

The court then pronounced sentence against her and imprisoned her for up to five weeks until the day came for her execution.

On that day Joane was taken to Windmill Hill Pit, her brother held her hand for support and comfort. A man called Dr Draicot gave a sermon at the execution site where he preached against the Reformers. He then declared that Joane Waste was a condemned heretic who would be presently consumed with fire in body and soul. Then with many terrible threats he concluded his sermon, and commanded that Joane Waste be burnt at the stake.

Joane's last words were prayers for mercy in the name of the Lord Jesus Christ. It was the first day of August 1556 and at just twenty-two years of age she breathed her last. However, even as the flames took the last of her life away, she could see more clearly than any of her accusers. And at the moment of her death she could see the face of the Lord Jesus Christ she had come to love and trust.

LOOK IT UP

1. Conviction – what does this word mean? Look it up in a dictionary and find out.

2. Do you see many examples of conviction in the world around you? Do you think people show more or less conviction today than in the past?

3. Think about how conviction can be true or false. Sometimes people can be convinced they are right when they are in fact wrong. You could interchange the word conviction with faith. We are told that faith is something that is given to us by God. Now look up these verses to find out about true conviction and faith and remember it's not about us having great faith – but it is about us having faith in a great God: Ephesians 2:8; Mark 11:22; Hebrews 11:1; 2 Peter 1:19; Romans 5:1-2; 2 Corinthians 5:7.

MARIA DE BOHORQUES
The Spanish Maiden

The Spanish Inquisition has gone down in history as a time of great terror and violence. Many people lost their lives during that time for a variety of reasons. Most lost their lives over issues of religion. The inquisition itself started in the 1400s, but was still going strong in the 1600s. Many people were attacked and tortured during this time. However, by the time the 1600s arrived this also included Protestants.

Here is a quote from one man who witnessed those times, 'In Spain, many very learned, many very noble, and many of the highest gentry, have for this cause' (that of the Reformed faith) 'been led forth to the scaffold.'

'There is not a city ... not a village, nor a hamlet, nor a noble house in Spain, that has not had one or more that God has enlightened with the light of his gospel. Our enemies have done what they could to put out this light, yet the more they threaten, scourge, throw into the galleys, imprison, or burn, the more they multiply.'

How was such a staunch Roman Catholic country reached with the good news of Jesus Christ? The chief tool that Christians used was literature. Throughout the Inquisition tracts and Bibles were printed. The Roman Catholic powers did all they could to prevent these from entering the country, but many books made it through and were gladly purchased by all classes.

One of the cities in which the gospel was preached was Seville – a wealthy city famous for its palaces, churches and ancient dwellings.

However, one building stood out from the others. Anyone who passed it would see its gloomy walls and iron-barred windows and realise that they were passing a prison. If you were a native of Seville you would also know that it was the court of the Inquisition. Within these walls tribunals were set up to inquire into the opinions of those who spoke against the Roman Catholic Church.

A group of monks known as *Inquisitors* sought out any who spoke against the Pope. These men were responsible for the deaths of many Reformed believers.

The Inquisitors had assistants who were called *Familiars*. Often these men were used to hunt down the Protestants or anyone else the church wished to imprison. Nobody did anything about it. If you stood up for a neighbour or tried to help a family member escape it might be you on their hit list next time. The power that these men held over the population was incredible. They could even get a husband to inform against his wife, or a parent against a child. Anyone who was even suspected of having read, or lent, or kept in their house a book of the Reformed faith would be thrown into the cells of the Inquisition court. It was enough simply to have a Protestant as a friend. So many chose their friends carefully.

Unfortunately one young Spanish lady, named Maria de Bohorques, found herself on the wrong side of the Inquisition. She was a well-connected member of the Spanish aristocracy and a member of a very noble family. The wealth and privileges of her early life were great. But as a young girl she did not set her heart on these things, but instead found herself being drawn towards her Lord and Saviour Jesus Christ. She was a beautiful young girl with a promising life ahead of her – but her faith meant far more than the pleasures of her noble life.

When Maria was about twenty-one years of age she was accused of being faithless to the Church of Rome. Her tutor, Doctor Gil, had become a Reformer and had carefully taught his young student from the Holy Bible. It didn't take her long to realise that what the Roman Catholic religion was teaching was against the truth of God. What is even more amazing is that

Maria had the courage to express her convictions out loud.

Maria knew about the Inquisition so she knew the risk that she was taking. She certainly wasn't a naïve young woman with no knowledge of what she was getting herself into. She knew that for as long as she continued to speak up for her faith she was in danger of being hauled up in front of the Inquisition. Indeed she could very well lose her life. Eventually that day did come. On the day of her trial Maria prayed to God for strength to face those who would judge her.

Silently she was led by the Familiars to a secret chamber, where the Inquisitors sat clad in dark robes, their faces hidden. They spoke softly to her at first hoping to persuade her gently to forget her faith. But as she listened to them Maria continued to pray in her heart that she would remain faithful. Boldly she confessed to the Inquisitors that she trusted in the Lord Jesus Christ alone for her salvation. Her judges then declared that, unless she submitted to the Church of Rome, she should be tried by torture.

The sight of the various instruments that they would use to inflict pain on her body did nothing to shake her faith in the truth. And even when that pain became a reality she refused to give her torturers the names of other Reformers.

Maria simply refused to renounce her faith or betray other believers. No mercy was shown to the young woman even though she pleaded with persecutors to show pity.

Eventually when the pain became too much Maria let slip that her sister, Juana, was also a secret follower of the Reformed faith. Juana was tortured in the same way as Maria, but did not survive. Maria was then sentenced to be burned as a heretic. Priest after priest was sent to her cell in order to get the young woman to convert back to the Church of Rome. However, Maria would not be persuaded. Instead she tried to teach them the truth of Scripture.

On 24 September 1559, many believers were burned at the stake and among them was Maria de Bohorques. Unable to walk she was carried to the place of execution by one of the Familiars. Above the noise and tumult of the crowd you could just about hear her singing as she stood ready for death.

Final attempts were made to make her renounce her faith. They asked to her to recite the creed – which she did – only she would stop every now and then to explain the true Reformed meaning of its message.

The final decision was then made. Maria de Bohorques was sentenced to death. Her nobility and wealth could not save her – but she had never assumed that they would. She was safe in the knowledge that her salvation had already been purchased by the death of her Saviour – and now she was going to meet him at last.

LOOK IT UP

1. Gospel – What does this word mean? Look it up in a dictionary and find out.

2. Maria and her sister were willing to die for their faith. Do you think you could do the same? What do you think about what Maria did when she let the inquisitors know about her sister?

3. Maria was given strength to stand up for her convictions – even though the inquisitors tricked her into betraying her sister. Look up the following Bible verses which refer to strength: Psalm 28:7-8; Psalm 46:1; Psalm 73:26; 1 Corinthians 1:25

ALICE BENDEN
Betrayed by her family

Can you picture a typical family home in the 1500s? The people living there are neither rich nor are they poor. They live well enough to feed their family from a full larder. They have enough money to keep the house warm with plenty of logs on the fire. Their clothes are clean and respectable. Every morning they pull fresh water from the well to wash with. They may not be rich, but they make sure their family are clean and well fed.

Now picture what it was like for Alice Benden. She was thrown into a prison for weeks on end with no change of clothing, no soap or fresh water to wash herself with. The basics that she had depended on before were taken away from her. And even those she'd loved and looked after deserted her.

Alice Benden was not a noble woman. She did not have wealthy possessions or connections at court. But she wasn't a beggar either. She was one of those women who probably assumed that she would live out her days working in her home, tending to her family and putting her husband's meals on the table.

However, for this normal 16th century housewife life was not going to be what she had imagined. On the 14th of October 1556, she was brought before Master Roberts of Cranbrooke, in the county of Kent. Alice Benden was a Protestant and believed that the mass celebrated by the church at that time was idolatrous.

When she was asked why she didn't attend the church services she replied, 'Because there is much idolatry committed against the glory of God there.'

Her answer put her in prison for fourteen days after which she was summoned before the Bishop of Dover.

'Have you now been persuaded to go home and go to the church?' he asked 'Will you now go to the priest to receive confession?'

Alice replied that she would not. Her answer was quite clear. However, the Bishop assumed that if he let her go home she would eventually change her position.

'Go thy ways home,' he said 'and go to the church when thou will.'

Anne was quiet and said nothing, but a priest who had attended her hearing declared, 'She promises she will, my lord.'

So she was set free and returned home.

However, when she got home it was a different matter. Married life for Alice was difficult to say the least. Her husband was a committed Roman Catholic. When he asked her to go to the church, she refused and nothing he could say would persuade her to change her mind.

A fortnight later Alice overheard some news that no wife should ever have to hear. 'Is it true that Alice Benden's husband has agreed to hand her to the constable if he'll pay him for his trouble?'

What a truly shameful thing to hear about your husband. But Alice knew what kind of man her husband was. He certainly had no care for what his neighbours thought. However, Alice Benden did care – she cared about her husband deeply and did not want him to be the disgrace of the town. So she gave herself up to the constable and was imprisoned in Canterbury Castle.

Now prison in those days was a dreadful ordeal. No provision was made for the inmates. If you had no blanket to warm yourself you had to purchase or steal one. If you had no food you did the same. Very few prisoners had any money with which to buy the necessities of life. But Alice and her cell mate had a little money given to them by Alice's brother who was also a Protestant. With this money they set themselves a budget of twopence halfpenny a day. They believed that they could make it stretch for quite some time if they kept to this plan.

In December Alice was removed from Canterbury Castle to the Bishop's prison. While she was there her husband arrived to plead for her liberty. However, the Bishop declared that she was so obstinate a heretic that he could not under any circumstances set her free.

'But my lord,' Benden exclaimed, 'if you just kept her brother, Roger Hall, from her. Without his influence she would recant. It is he who supplies her with the little money that she has and persuades her not to relent.'

The Bishop promised to do something about the situation and so Alice's husband left. But Alice was not given her freedom as her husband had hoped. Instead the Bishop gave instructions to put her into a prison called Monday's Hole. If her brother was seen anywhere nearby he was to be instantly apprehended.

Monday's Hole was a terrible prison. Most prisons at that time were horrendous places, but this one capped the lot. It was the cruelest prison of all. Built underground the entrance to the prison was protected by a five foot fence. This made it impossible for anyone to get near enough to speak to a prisoner without being overheard.

When Alice first arrived there she could not understand how God had allowed this to happen.

However, verses of scripture and the promises of God came back to her memory.

The promise that 'The right hand of the Most High can change all,' brought her comfort and peace.

The conditions in the prison were far worse than before. Her bed was a few handfuls of straw thrown on the floor, and she was only allowed three farthings a day for food. With that money she was allowed to buy a halfpenny loaf and a farthing drink, but nothing more. Alice pleaded with her jailor to allow her to use the rest of her money to purchase something else to eat or drink. But he refused.

Now Alice's location was not known to any of her family as she had been removed from the last prison secretly. Very few people knew of the Monday's Hole so any efforts to find her were unsuccessful. However, after she had been in the dungeon about five weeks her brother happened to be passing by early in the morning. Alice was singing a Psalm at the time and he heard her.

Because her gaoler was absent Alice's brother was able to speak to her for a few moments. He hid some money in a loaf of bread, which he stuck on a pole and passed over the fence to her.

Nine weeks went by before she was called before the Bishop and during that time she had been given no change of clothes. Imagine how loathsome and disgusting she must have felt. Those who had been called on to judge her must have seen how poorly clothed she was. They would have smelt the dirt of the prison on her skin. Fleas and lice would have been crawling over her rags.

As the Bishop looked at his prisoner he was certain that she must have had enough. 'Surely she will be only too glad to yield to our authority. '

He asked her if she would now go home and attend the church.

'I am thoroughly persuaded,' she replied, 'by the great extremity that you have already showed me, that you are not of God, neither can your doings be godly, and I see that you seek my utter destruction.'

The long confinement in the Monday's Hole had made her lame from the damp cold and lack of food. Alice was now no longer able to move without suffering great pain. During her next imprisonment in Westgate her skin completely peeled off as if it had been poisoned. After her next tribunal Alice was imprisoned in the Castle until 19 June 1557. It was then that she met the same death as many of her fellow believers when she burned to death at the stake.

LOOK IT UP

1. Glory – what does the word 'glory' mean? Look it up in a dictionary and find out.

2. Do you see many examples of glory in your day to day life? Do you see examples of people taking glory to themselves who do not deserve it?

3. Think about God's glory. Sometimes when people glorify themselves we see it as arrogant and selfish. Why is this not the case with God? Look up the following verses: Psalm 19:1; Psalm 29:2.

PREST'S WIFE
Her Name was Lost but she Wasn't

C an you imagine what it must be like to live in a country where you do not have the privilege of freedom? You can not even speak your mind in your own home and you are forbidden to express yourself, unless you express exactly what your rulers desire.

There are many countries like that today, but in the past countries that are known as democracies today were ruled by tyrants. Not all of these tyrants were men. Queen Mary has gone down in history with a particularly unpleasant nickname. 'Bloody Mary' got her name from the vast number of men and women who were put to the stake during her reign.

Vast numbers were martyred during that time. So it is no surprise to discover that many of the female martyrs from this era have disappeared with their names unrecorded and unacknowledged. They were without wealth or connection and had no one to remember their names. Many did not have the ability to record it for themselves. 'Prest's wife,' is one of those.

She would not have been able to read and would have had very little, if any, education. However, she did have a knowledge and understanding of God and his Word.

Her husband, Prest, was not rich and struggled to support his wife and children in their humble home near Launceston, England. Mrs Prest was a God-fearing woman, who earned her living by spinning. She often spoke out against the idolatrous and superstitious practices of the time. And when this became known it wasn't long before she was summoned to appear before the Bishop of Exeter to give an account of her conduct.

'You foolish woman,' declared the Bishop, 'I hear that you hath spoken words against the most blessed sacrament of the altar, the body of Christ. Shame! You art an unlearned person and a woman. Will you meddle with such high matters, which all the learned men of the world cannot define? And, if it be as I am informed, you art worthy to be burned.'

He then asked her what she had to say regarding the mass and she replied –'There never was such an idol as your sacrament is made of by your priests... Christ did command it to be eaten and drunken in remembrance of his most blessed passion, for our redemption.'

'See this prattling woman,' exclaimed the Bishop. 'Did not Christ say over the bread, 'This is my body,' and over the cup, 'This is my blood'?'

'Yes, indeed he said so, but he meant that it is his body and blood, not carnally, but sacramentally.'

'Alas, poor woman, you art deceived.'

'No, my lord, I am not deceived; and if you will give me leave, I will declare a reason why I will not worship the sacrament.'

'Say on; I'm sure it will be goodly.'

'Truly, goodly enough that I will lose this poor life of mine for.'

'Then you will be a martyr, good wife?'

'Indeed... I will suffer it with all my heart. Can you deny your creed, which says that Christ perpetually sits at the right hand of his Father, both body and soul until he comes again? He is there in heaven as our advocate, and makes prayer for us unto God his Father. If it be so, He is not here on the earth in a piece of bread.... If He did offer his body once for all, why do you make a new offering? If He is to be worshipped in spirit and truth, why do you worship a piece of bread? I know that I am but a poor woman; but I would rather live no longer than do as you do. I have said, sir.'

Her inquisitors were so astonished at her words that they thought she was insane. They persuaded the Bishop to let her have her freedom, but at the same time keeping her under observation. So she was handed over to the prison warden who made her his servant.

Mrs Prest, though under observation, was still allowed to go about wherever she pleased. The priests, however, did not give up on her. They continued to quiz her about her beliefs and tried to get her to recant. Mrs Prest declared that she would be ashamed to say that a piece of bread could be turned by a man into the natural body of Christ. 'Bread doth grow musty, and mice oftentimes do eat it. God's own body will not be so affected, nor kept in prison or in boxes. Let it be your God, it shall not be mine, for my Saviour sitteth on the right hand of God to intercede for me.'

After she had been in the warden's house for a few weeks she walked past a church where a man was mending the statues of the saints that had been broken.

'What a madman thou art,' she said, 'to make them new noses which within a few days shall all lose their heads.'

After those words she was, on the Bishop's orders, immediately cast into prison. From that time on she would be granted no liberty whatsoever. This poor, uneducated woman was, however, a great example to those who visited her. Many were astonished at her knowledge. Anyone who mentioned a passage of scripture would be told by Mrs Prest where it could be found in the Bible.

Eventually when the court told her of her impending death, Mrs Prest remained calm and resolute. She simply answered, 'With my death I am content to be a witness of Christ's death, and I pray you make no longer delay with me. My heart is fixed. I will never say otherwise, nor return to the old superstitions.'

The day of her execution arrived and while a chain was being fastened round her waist, and the flames being lit at her feet she cried aloud, 'God be merciful to me a sinner.' These were her last words.

LOOK IT UP

1. In a dictionary look up the definition of the word 'witness'. What does it mean?

2. Look out for the word witness in the news. What sort of story usually uses the word?

3. When Christians use the word witness they are talking about telling others about Christ or sticking up for the truth of God's Word. In Acts 1:8 the Christians were told that they would receive special help in order to be God's witnesses – what was this?

HELEN STARK
Joined in Life and in Death

Imagine you are a young mother looking after your children, making sure they are fed and well clothed, teaching them to read and write and live godly lives. You love your husband and you support him in his work. You lead a happy, steady life without much riches, but with plenty of joy and contentment. Then you are faced with what must be one of the greatest dilemmas for a Christian parent. You are accused of being a Christian and have to face the prospect of losing your home, livelihood and family. If you refuse to submit to the authorities you will see your children taken away to be brought up by others and you will face the death penalty.

Christian Heroines

This is what happened to the mother, Helen Stark, when during the reign of the infant queen, Mary Queen of Scots she was accused of belonging to the Reformed faith.

When James the Fifth of Scotland died an infant daughter, Mary, just a few days old was left as his successor. She would one day become the famous Mary Queen of Scots; but until she reached the age of maturity when she could reign in her own name a regency had to be appointed to carry on the affairs of the kingdom.

David Beatoun was a cunning and ambitious cardinal, who had been Prime Minister to the late king. He presented a parchment which claimed to be the last will and testament of James V. In it Beatoun was declared chief regent. It was exposed as a forgery, however, and the Earl of Arran was chosen to rule the kingdom.

Arran followed the Reformed religion, but his timid nature and weakness of leadership meant that he was not a good choice. The country was in turmoil and it needed a strong pair of hands – and there were plenty strong hands grasping to take power for themselves.

It wasn't long before Beatoun seized power and Arran was ruler in name only – completely under Beatoun's control.

At that point in history Scotland had what is referred to as religious liberty. Its people were allowed to worship as they wished. As well as that the people were permitted to read the Bible in their own language. Many Bibles were printed and read across Scotland. They were being read in crofts and school houses, cottages and castles. Both rich and poor were discovering the truths of God's Word for themselves. However, Beatoun was determined to put a stop to this, and so he began a very cruel persecution of the Protestants.

During one of his attempts to wipe out the Reformed Religion in Scotland, Beatoun visited Perth. The year was 1544 and at that time Perth was headquarters for very important Reformers.

Many of the inhabitants of that town were brought up before Beatoun's inquisition – but most were set free with a warning. Six people, however, were made an example of. Among these was a woman named Helen Stark and her husband.

The prisoners were accused of meeting together to discuss the Bible and Helen Stark was also accused of despising the church. This was because when she had fallen ill she had refused to call on the Virgin Mary to relieve her of her sickness. Her neighbours had begged her to do so, but Helen had replied that she would pray to God alone in the name of Christ.

All the prisoners were found guilty, and sentenced to death. The men were to be hanged while the women were to be drowned. Helen Stark's plea to be allowed to die with her husband was turned down. 'You may watch your husband perish,' they laughed and forced her to be witness at her own husband's death.

The inhabitants of Perth pleaded with the Cardinal for mercy, but he would not listen to their request for pardon. Many soldiers were put on duty that day as the authorities feared that friends and relatives would try to set the prisoners free.

Helen's thoughts, however, were not on a rescue, but on giving courage and strength to her husband. 'Be glad,' she said; 'we have lived together many joyful days, but this day on which we must die ought to be the most joyful of all to us both, because now we shall have joy for ever. Therefore I will not bid you goodbye, for we shall suddenly meet with joy in the kingdom of heaven.'

In Helen's arms lay a baby, only a few weeks old. She had other children too who were soon going to be orphans. At the gallows Mr Stark's death only took a few moments. With a quick glance at the body of her husband, Helen Stark was moved towards a local pool which was just a little distance away.

With a few words and a kiss to each of her children she entrusted them to the care of her neighbours. The executioner then bound Helen's hands and feet, thrust her into a sack and threw her into the water.

Minutes later the pond was totally calm. Helen Stark had experienced a terrible death, but now the peace and joy she had spoken about with her husband was hers.

LOOK IT UP

1. In a dictionary look up the definition of the word 'joy'. What does it mean?

2. What things make you joyful? What events are usually associated with great joy?

3. Look up the following Bible verses to find the true secret of real joy: Psalm 19:8; Psalm 21:6; Psalm 51:12; Psalm 92:4; James 1:2-3.

THE COVENANTERS

The struggle for a biblical church and pure worship continued even after Great Britain was considered a Protestant country. In reality the church was controlled by the Crown and the Bible was still banished from the home. This became the time of the Covenanters and stretched from the 1630s through to the 1670s until Prince William of Orange made a bloodless invasion of Great Britain in 1688.

Men and women from both Scotland and England faced severe repression for their stand against the established church and their faith in Christ as the only head of the Church. They were the Covenanters.

There was some relief under Oliver Cromwell when the United Kingdom became a republic very briefly. King Charles I was beheaded after the Civil War but his son was restored to the throne in 1660 and the persecutions began once more.

As often happens in situations like this the Covenanters were forced to take up arms against the king and his organised troops. As political and religious upheaval spanned the country many Bible-believing Christians were sent to their deaths. The women sadly were defenceless and many did not even receive a proper trial. Yet some like Margaret Wilson went to their deaths praying for their enemies and the salvation of their king and murderer.

THINGS TO DO:

1. Find out what the word 'covenant' means.

2. Visit websites that belong to Christian organisations supporting the world wide church such as Voice of the Martyrs and Christian Solidarity Worldwide. What examples can you see of Christian persecution today? Do you feel as though Christians are persecuted in your country?

3. Take out an atlas and look up the location of any place that is mentioned in the stories.

ELIZABETH WELCH
Fearless and Faithful

Who is the most powerful ruler in your country? Do they have a worldwide repuation? Does their name appear on news bulletins and web pages? Imagine how you would feel then if you had to approach this person in order to plead for your freedom or the freedom of your family. You would be ushered into their presence to make your speech. Your knees would be knocking and your heart hammering inside your chest. You are just a little person in their eyes and of no consequence. They wield the power – and you can do nothing. How would you feel if they mocked at you and failed to take you seriously?

In the 1600s those who held the most power were monarchs. In what we now call the United Kingdom James VI of Scotland had secured his succession to the English throne. It wasn't long before he began to bring the Church of Scotland into conformity with the Church of England. What was the difference between these two denominations?

Well, the Church in Scotland was Presbyterian meaning that the congregations were governed by the ministers and elders of these congregations. These men were called Presbyters. The Presbyterian churches had no bishops in charge. All of its ministers were equals. The church courts were elected by the members of the Church. Christ alone was regarded as the Head of the Church.

Now, for James VI this caused a problem. He could have very little influence over an organisation like this. He was King of England so surely he could do whatever he wanted? However, as the Presbyterian Church was popular with the people in Scotland this meant that the King's power over the people was diminished. So it was ruled that the Church was to be deprived of her General Assemblies.

These were the conferences held by the Church during which vital decisions were made regarding the future and the teaching of the denomination. However, the Presbyterians paid no heed to the King's decree and met anyway in Aberdeen. James was furious and commanded them to give up their meeting. At the same time he arrested fourteen of the ministers.

This is where we are introduced to one particular individual named John Welch. He was the minister of Ayr, and a bold and fearless gentleman. John was keen to stand up for the rights of the Scottish Church and would not give in to the arrogant demands of the monarch. He was the husband of Elizabeth Knox who was the daughter of John Knox – that well known theologian.

Many would have seen John Welch as a good match for Elizabeth Knox. However, it wasn't always the case. As a young man he had been rebellious and disobedient. Many times he ran away from school, but was brought back with strict instructions to behave himself. However, there was one day when his family thought they had lost him forever. He ran away and could not be found because he had joined a gang of thieves.

However, John Welch soon realised that his dreams of excitement and adventure were foolish and vain. Soon his clothes turned to rags and the poverty and hunger he had afflicted upon himself sent him home with his tail between his legs.

The homecoming wasn't easy. John's father had been very hurt by his son's actions, but eventually they were reconciled and John was pardoned. It wasn't just his father's pardon that he received. John humbly sought the pardon of God through his Son Jesus Christ. The young man who would have become a robber became a reformer instead. And it was this that brought John Welch into the clutches of James VI and his henchmen. Because of his refusal to bow down to the demands of his monarch John Welch was placed under arrest and taken to the jail in Linlithgow.

When Elizabeth heard of his arrest she left her children in the care of some friends and set off to find her husband immediately.

The conditions at that time of year were not good for travelling. It was January 1605 and a bitter cold wind and heavy snowfalls made it very difficult for Elizabeth to make any headway. Thankfully, despite the terrible weather, Elizabeth reached Linlithgow. However, she was exhausted from the journey.

On arrival in the town she discovered that John and his companions had been charged with high treason. It was a sentence punishable by death... yet Elizabeth did not weep. She was only thankful that her husband had been given the strength to remain faithful – even unto death.

However, the sentence was to be carried out at the King's pleasure so there was a delay and the prisoners were put back into the dungeons. It turned out that the King was not sure what to do with the prisoners. He didn't want to free them, but he didn't want to kill them either. If he carried out the death penalty it would make him very unpopular. Eventually King James banished the ministers from the country and told them never again to return on pain of death.

On 23 October the men were ordered to depart into exile for France within the month. On 7 November the exiles boarded a ship at Leith while tearful wives and family waved them farewell.

Elizabeth watched her husband's ship disappear on the horizon. She may have been heartbroken, but she was also determined to follow him before the year was out.

John's voyage to France was not an easy one – heavy winds caused the boat to rise and fall erratically, but after some time they finally arrived and John Welch stayed first at Rochelle and then Bordeaux before settling in Jousack as a minister to a congregation there.

It was in Jousack that his wife and family found him in great poverty. The church members there showed no sympathy or care for their pastor and did little to alleviate his suffering. Perhaps when his wife and family arrived they would be more compassionate? Not so! A letter written on the 17 September 1611 describes their dreadful situation.

'We are here in a miserable hole, without pity or compassion, among as it were barbarians. Notwithstanding that our lodging be such for unwholesomeness, that ever since I came here my family have been sick, yet they would never show me that much favour as to provide a lodging that was suitable for my health and the health of my family. The indignities I receive, and have received here, are intolerable; but I have learned to bear them for Christ's sake. My wife has been sick of a continual fever this month or more.'

Despite all these trials and difficulties Elizabeth continued to serve her husband and family with an inward strength of character that showed great patience and heroism.

John himself was heard to utter 'I thank God that my wife bears her cross with content, the which to me is no small comfort.'

However, the family suffered greatly from poor health. Their eldest daughter died after a brief illness and Mr Welch was so sick afterwards that it seemed as though there was nothing that could be done. In a desperate attempt to bring some measure of health back to her family Elizabeth moved them to the South of France to a better climate. But even there her husband was struck down with a lung disease. When they travelled to Zealand, an island off the coast of Denmark, the doctor there suggested that it might be better to take John back to Scotland. 'At least he would be in the land that he loves.'

John Welch wrote to King James for permission to return to England. He secretly hoped that soon after that he would be allowed to return to Scotland. King James eventually agreed to let the Welch family return to England and soon they were living in London. But London wasn't Scotland and that was where John had a real desire to be. However, John was too frail and sick to plead any further with James VI. So he sent Elizabeth in his stead to attend a personal meeting with the King.

She personally appealed to the monarch to allow John to return to Scotland. She was allowed access into the royal throne room and was presented to the

King of the realm. However, when he was told that she was the wife of John Welch and the daughter of John Knox, King James scowled darkly.

'Knox and Welch, a pretty alliance indeed,' he growled.

The interview wasn't altogether pleasant and in the end the King would only allow John to travel to Scotland if he submitted himself to the bishops. 'If he agrees to that then he can go.'

Even John Knox's daughter, Elizabeth, turned and steadily met the monarch's iron gaze. Taking her apron in her hands she lifted it up and held it in front of him.

'Please, your Majesty, I'd rather receive his head in this.'

Mrs Welch was then duly dismissed. Her attempt to move the King of the realm had amounted to nothing. John did not live for much longer. He was finally buried in a London churchyard. Elizabeth, however, did manage to return to Scotland.

LOOK IT UP

1. Many Christians have suffered exile over the years. Look up the word 'exile' in the dictionary. What does it mean?

2. John Knox was well known for being strong and committed. In what ways did Elizabeth show similar characteristics?

3. What does the Bible say to people who are exiles or who cannot for a while live in the homes that they want to? 2 Peter 3:13, John 14:23, Hebrews 11:8-10.

MARION FAIRLIE
Suffering in Separation

Imagine that you are woken in the early hours of the morning by soldiers breaking into your house. Your children are crying in the stairway as your husband is manhandled out of the door. He is to be taken to a prison, hundreds of miles away – and you may never see him again. This is what happened to Marion Fairlie when her husband was arrested for preaching the gospel. She was practically left destitute – with no money and no one to help her in her difficulties.

Marion Fairlie didn't endure a martyr's death as many in this book have done – but we can certainly say that she was familiar with persecution.

When she was twenty-six years of age, Marion became engaged to a minister named William Veitch against the advice of many of her friends.

'Why do you insist on marrying a minister, dear girl?' an interfering neighbour exclaimed. 'King Charles is trying his utmost to force an Episcopal government on the Scottish church. And we all know what will happen if he gets his way. She who marries a minister in these days need look for little save straits and oppression and poverty, with death as the only escape.'

But despite the doleful predictions Marion remained firm and resolute. She would not be swayed by her friends, but instead followed her heart and became Mrs William Veitch.

However, not long into their marriage these troubles did in fact come to pass.

Ministers who refused to conform to what the King demanded were turned out of their livings. These men and their families became penniless wanderers whose chapels were the storm blown hills and whose pulpits were the rocks and burns where their faithful congregations might come and listen to their preaching in secret.

If you attended these meetings, or conventicles as they were called, you risked your very life as men like Sir James Turner made it their business in life to root out the Covenanters and torture them cruelly. Many who attended these meetings instead of going to the Parish churches lost their lives because of it.

It became too much for some of the Covenanters and they rose in revolt, organising a protest march to Edinburgh. William Veitch was among them. However, as they marched towards Edinburgh the King's troops overtook them at the Pentland Hills.

Veitch fled and despite great dangers eventually made it to a friend's house which wasn't that far from his own home. A message was sent to Marion to inform her that all was well. At which she breathed a sigh of relief. If he had decided to return home he might have ran straight into a troop of soldiers who had arrived that day to make a thorough search of the house. No doubt they had hoped to find William in some hiding place.

The following morning Marion instructed a friend to ride with her to the house of the Rev. Patrick Fleming at Stobo. On the way she kept a sharp lookout for search parties, but seeing none she sent a message back to her husband that the road was clear and safe for him to travel on.

That night William arrived at Stobo where he was fed and watered, but instructed to seek shelter elsewhere. Stobo wasn't safe enough. It was too close to where the troops had been searching. 'If you and Mrs Veitch head for the borders that might be far enough. You could find shelter there and lie low for a while,' he was advised. However, when William and Marion discovered that William's name was on a list of wanted men they decided that he must flee to England. William said goodbye to his faithful wife and headed for Newcastle. Marion meanwhile returned to her home in the Westhills of Dunsyre. However, a few weeks later a crowd of troopers arrived at her door demanding that she let them in. They had come to search for her husband. Night after night they came and went – but of course they found nothing.

William heard of the danger his wife was in and immediately set out to return to Scotland. When he arrived he helped Marion to pack up their belongings, sell the house and land and then set up home in Edinburgh. It was there that she lived peacefully until 1672, when William became minister at Reedsdale, in Northumberland and Marion finally became reunited with her husband after eight long years.

Sometime after that William moved his family to Stantonhall, a few miles from Morpeth where they also farmed a small piece of ground. This was one way to make sure he could feed his growing family and keep them out of the clutches of poverty. It was a peaceful time where the couple were very happy. But Veitch's preaching soon attracted notice and attempts were made to apprehend him.

One Lord's Day afternoon, about three o'clock, two justices and a party of soldiers broke into the house with pistols in hand. They went from room to room, turning over furniture, opening wardrobes and chests, looking under beds. But moments before they had gained entry William had hidden behind some curtains in a large window. Strangely enough none of the soldiers thought to look there and when they couldn't find him left the house disgruntled. However, as they left they warned Mrs Veitch to tell her husband that he must stop his unlawful preaching or else!

William, however, would not submit to the authorities demands. So at about five o'clock one morning an officer with a party of dragoons surrounded the Veitches house. There was no time to escape and William was arrested, taken to Morpeth Gaol in order to be sent back to Scotland.

This was what Mrs Veitch feared the most. As soon as she heard she set out for Morpeth to bid him farewell. It was midnight and in the middle of a blizzard when she reached the town. She only had a few moments to speak to her husband before he was taken away to Edinburgh.

Because William had to pay for his own expenses in prison, Marion was forced to sell most of the farm stock. This meant that she and her family had virtually nothing to live on. Even the crops that had been planted were now ruined, because there was no one to work the land, and no animals to do it with.

Friends and neighbours did what they could to help the young family so that even in the midst of their poverty Marion was sure of one thing – her gracious, Heavenly Father would not cast them off. She trusted him implicitly and believed that everything – both good and bad – was for the best.

In February 1679 William wrote to her to ask her to come to Edinburgh as soon as she could. There was a hope that he might be released from prison very shortly. Marion immediately organised care for the children and set off on what was a perilous journey.

It was very rare for a woman to travel on her own in those days. Marion would have had many concerns as she made her way North. Highwaymen and other ruffians were one of the many risks that travellers had to face. Bad roads and severe weather made it both dangerous and uncomfortable. Eventually Marion reached the capital despite the horrendous snow storm she had to tackle. However, just as she thought her husband would be released Marion was horrified to hear that he had to appear before the Justiciary Court. They had discovered that he had been accused of treason twelve years ago. William was to face the death sentence.

However, there were delays and William remained in prison until the month of July when he was finally released without charge.

William and Marion returned to their home in Stantonhall – but it was with some regret that they left their native land of Scotland. Both husband and wife longed to be able to return in freedom and this was what they fervently prayed for.

God answered that prayer in 1685 when after the Revolution the Veitches were able to move to Peebles and then to Dumfries. Both William and Marion died in the year 1722 – barely a day separated Marion's death from her husband's.

LOOK IT UP

1. What does the word 'trust' mean? Look it up in a dictionary.

2. What kind of people do you trust? If you were to go through a list of people that you thought it was safe to trust what sort of people would they be? What characteristics would they have in common?

3. In Proverbs 3:4-6 we are told to trust in God? How do we do this? Is that always easy? When we do this what will happen? Read Romans 10:11; Romans 15:13.

ISABEL ALISON
A Single Girl is Single Minded

In the future do you think your country will be famous for something? Perhaps it will be engineering or medical advances? Maybe great discoveries will be made because of the people who live in the place you call home. But can you imagine what it would be like to live in a country that is famous for something bad. At one point in the country of Scotland there were so many killings people began to call those years 'The Killing Years'?

It was during those years that a young woman, Isabel Alison, lived and loved. In her twenties, Isabel was a single girl from Perth and one day she spoke her mind as young women often do. She couldn't believe how harshly the Covenanters were being treated. Almost as soon as she had spoken the words, the young woman was taken before the magistrates. However, there wasn't enough evidence to convict her so she was let go with a warning.

Isabel, however, paid little heed to the warning and continued to live her life as she had done before the trial. A large part of her life at that time was attending the field conventicles to hear the Bible being preached and the gospel proclaimed. Whenever there was a meeting, she would do her utmost to attend it.

However, there were people watching her movements now. Isabel was a marked woman. It wasn't long before she was arrested once again by the orders of the Privy Council and taken to a prison in Edinburgh. Why was a young, law abiding woman thrown in prison? She was simply known as a Covenanter and her captors wanted the names of other Covenanters. But what was the problem with Covenanters?

Well, to sum it up briefly the Covenanters were part of a movement in Scotland which supported the development of a Presbyterian church in Scotland rather than an Episcopal church, which was favoured by the Crown. The Covenanters signed the National Covenant in 1638 in order to confirm their opposition to the interference by the Stuart kings in the Scottish church.

These kings believed that they had a divine right to rule and that they were infallible. They also believed that they were the spiritual heads of the Church of

Scotland. Those who were for a Presbyterian form of government believed that there was only one head of the church – Jesus Christ.

In the year 1637, King Charles I introduced the Book of Common Prayer to Scotland. This new liturgy was widely opposed throughout the country. But the King declared that any opposition to it would be treason and punished by death.

The ministers who would not submit to the King's authority were thrown out of their churches. That was when the conventicles began. These open air meetings were attended by thousands of people. At other times only handfuls could make their way into the mountains to worship in secret and freedom.

However, citizens who did not attend their local churches could face heavy fines. They were accused of being rebels and often questioned under torture. But as often happens in times of political upheaval our heroes can be seen to have flaws. Though the Covenanters were in the right to stand up for religious liberties – some were forced into committing crimes that they should not have done.

Just one year before Isabel's trial the Archbishop of St Andrews had been killed on Magus Moor by a small group of Covenanters. They had been persecuted relentlessly by the Bishop and had rashly decided to take the law into their own hands. As a result punishment was dealt out to many more Presbyterians. At their trials they would often be asked the question, 'Was the killing of the Bishop of St Andrews a pious act?'

On 6 December 1680, Isabel was brought before the Lords of the Privy Council on charges of High Treason. She too was asked if she thought the slaying of Archbishop Sharp was a pious act.

'If it pleases the Lord to raise up men to execute his just judgments I have nothing to say against it,' she replied.

Her judges were furious.

'Do you disown us, and the King's authority in us?'

'I disown you all,' she cried fearlessly, 'because you carry the sword against God and not for him.'

One judge advised her to be careful, as her very life depended on the answers she gave.

'Would ye have me to lie?' Isabel replied. 'I would not quit one truth though it would purchase my life a thousand years, which you cannot purchase or promise for an hour.'

Isabel was then questioned about whether she had seen or spoken with any of the men suspected of the murder of Archbishop Sharp. At first she refused to answer, but eventually she admitted that she had.

'Then your blood be upon your own head. We shall be free of it,' her judges declared.

Isabel was then taken back to prison. On 17 January 1681 she was brought before a jury, charged with receiving, maintaining, supplying, and keeping company with the murderers of Archbishop Sharp. On the 21st she was condemned to death.

Isabel was to be taken to the Grassmarket of Edinburgh 'upon Wednesday next, the 29th betwixt the hours of two and four o'clock in the afternoon, and there to be hanged on a gibbet till she be dead, and all her goods and gear to be forfeited for the King's use.'

A courageous and faithful young woman she remained calm as her sentence was read out. The following extract from one of her letters from prison sheds light on her peace of mind: "Therefore let my enemies and pretended friends say what they will, I could have my life on no easier terms than denying Christ's kingly office. So I lay down my life for owning and adhering to Jesus Christ, who is a free King in his own house; and I bless the Lord that ever He called me to that."

On the day of her execution she sang the eighty-fourth Psalm and read the sixteenth chapter of Mark. At the scaffold she prayed briefly and then mounted the ladder – a moment later and her earthly life was over, but the best life with Jesus Christ in heaven, was beginning.

Perhaps one day you will visit the churchyard at Wigton to see the memorial tablet which was set up to record the manner of their death. There is also a monument to the Two Margarets in the Church of Holy Rude in the town of Stirling. It is important not to forget these women and others like them – but it is even more important not to forget the truths they died for and the God they served.

LOOK IT UP

1. Authority – look up the word in a dictionary and find out what it means.

2. In your day to day life what people have authority over you? Is it always right to obey those who are in authority over you? To find out what the Bible says look up Romans 13:1; Hebrews 13:17.

3. The Bible tells us that the true authority of Jesus Christ is a different authority to what we see in the world. Read the following verses: Matthew 20:24-26; Matthew 28:18.

4. Here are two verses from Psalm 84 that Margaret Wilson sang before she died. What do these words tell us about Margaret's heart and mind at that point?

1 How lovely is thy dwelling-place,
   O Lord of hosts, to me!
   The tabernacles of thy grace
   how pleasant, Lord, they be!

2 My thirsty soul longs veh'mently,
   yea faints, thy courts to see:
   My very heart and flesh cry out,
   O living God, for thee.

MARION HERVEY
A Scots Maid

If you had been alive during 'The Killing Time' would you have attended the conventicles? Would you have gone along to a meeting just out of curiosity? What would you have thought about those people who were willing to risk their lives in order to worship in the way that they thought was right? Would you have admired them for their faithfulness or advised them not to antagonise the authorities? Perhaps you would have respected them for their bravery – but turned away whenever you were called on to show courage? The reality is that there were indeed many courageous men, women and children who threw in their lot with the Covenanters. These people came from all walks of life. Marion Hervey came from the ranks of what we might now call the working class. She was a servant girl who was called on not only to serve God with her life – but also with her death.

While Isabel Alison was preparing for her execution Marion Hervey was to face the same sentence along with her.

Marion was just about twenty years of age. She had been brought up to attend her local episcopal church, but one day she decided to attend a conventicle simply out of curiosity.

Over time she became deeply impressed by the faith of the Covenanters, and decided to join them. Shortly afterwards, however, when on her way to attend a meeting she was taken prisoner by a party of soldiers.

On being brought before the Privy Council she underwent the same examination as Isabel Alison, and showed the same undaunted courage.

When the test question was put to her, 'Do you consider the slaying of Archbishop Sharp a pious act?' she replied – 'In so far as the Lord raised up instruments to execute his last judgements upon him, I have nothing to say against it, for he was a perjured wretch and a betrayer of the cause.'

She was then sent back to prison to await a trial by jury. When the men who would declare her innocent or guilty took their places, she stood up and announced in a loud voice, 'Beware what you are doing, for they have nothing to say against me, but only for owning Jesus Christ and his persecuted truths.'

Her prosecutors took no heed of her warning and a verdict of guilty was returned. She was then sentenced to be hanged in the Grassmarket along with Isabel Alison.

Her last words, spoken as she stood on the scaffold with a noose around her neck, were about how she believed Christ was Lord of all, 'I come here today for avowing Christ to be Head of the Church and King in Zion.'

LOOK IT UP

1. Trial – what does this word mean?

2. Where would you usually see the word trial used in newspaper cuttings and what people are usually involved in stories like these?

3. Can you name two famous people from the New Testament who were put on trial and then sentenced to death.

MARGARET WILSON

A Solway Firth Martyr

Imagine that you are standing a short distance away from the Solway Firth. You've just arrived as the tide is going out and before you there is a large flat plane of sand with rivulets of water here and there. In the distance you spot a stone pillar beyond the sandbanks. You think about investigating it further, but it's a cold Scottish day in the borders so you decide to go and see if Wigton has a nice tea room that you can shelter in for an hour or so. Some time later you make your way back to the same view you saw when you first arrived – but now there is quite a different scene. The water is high and the pillar has almost disappeared. If you know the story of the Two Margarets then you'll know that the scene you are now looking at is what Margaret Wilson's family would have witnessed on the day the young teenager was forcibly tied to a stake in the Solway Firth and drowned. Another Covenanter punished by her King for her faith.

The Killing Time, as it was called, was a period of terrible oppression for Covenanters. It is said that if anyone was found reading the Bible they were shot on sight. No mercy was shown to age or sex.

This was the background to Margaret Wilson's life. Her family owned prosperous farm land near Wigton and Margaret's parents regularly attended the local parish church. However, Margaret and her sister, Agnes, were Covenanters and would not attend the parish services, no matter how much their parents begged them.

Both Margaret and Agnes knew what the dangers were, but they would not give up attending the open air worship services held by the Covenanters.

The Wigton magistrates soon heard of this and a raid was made on the family home. Margaret and Agnes managed to escape, however, and the two girls fled for the hills.

The officers were furious when they discovered that their prey had escaped and forbad Mr and Mrs Wilson to offer any shelter to their children or provide them with food or warm clothing. If either of them discovered where their children were hiding they were to tell the authorities immediately.

Margaret and Agnes lived in the hills with other Covenanters for quite some time, but when Charles the Second passed away the two girls decided that it was safe to return to Wigton to visit their friends.

They were both keen to find out how Margaret MacLachlan was doing and set out towards her house. However, before they arrived they met a man named Patrick Stuart. By the way he spoke you would have thought that he was sympathetic towards the Covenanters. Margaret and Agnes certainly thought so until he asked them to drink the King's health. The two girls refused and immediately continued on their journey. Patrick Stuart, however, informed the magistrates about the girls' presence in the town and before the day was out both girls were thrown into Wigton Gaol. On the following Sunday, Margaret MacLachlan was also imprisoned.

Eventually all three were brought before the magistrates, and charged with having attended conventicles, refusing the administrations of the curate, and having been among the rebels at the Battle of Bothwell Bridge.

The final accusation was simply ridiculous for when the battle was fought Margaret was only twelve years of age, and her sister about eight.

After a mockery of a trial, sentence was pronounced that on the 11 May they should be, "tied to stakes fixed within the flood mark in the water of Blednoch, near Wigton, where the sea flows at high water, there to be drowned."

Margaret and Agnes' father hurried to Edinburgh in an attempt to save their lives. Eventually, Agnes was set free because she was under sixteen years of age. However, Mr Wilson had to pay one hundred pounds sterling for her release – a huge sum for a farmer in those days.

Mr Wilson continued to try and gain pardon for his eldest daughter, but on 11 May 1685 the two Margarets, one a teenager and one an elderly woman, were led out of prison by a troop of soldiers.

A great crowd of people stood round the little bay which opens into the Solway. Margaret MacLachlan was tied to the stake nearest to the water's edge, so that the younger woman might see her sufferings and possibly beg for forgiveness and give up her principles.

Slowly the tide came in until eventually the old woman was completely covered.

'What think ye of what ye see?" said one of the soldiers to Margaret Wilson.

'What do I see,' she replied, 'but Christ in one of his members wrestling there. Think you that we are the sufferers? No, it is Christ in us, for He sends none a warfare upon their own charges.'

The tide increased in speed, but the young Margaret remained calm while in a clear sweet voice she sang verses of the twenty-fifth Psalm.

My sins and faults of youth
Do Thou, O Lord, forget.
After Thy mercy think on me,
And for Thy goodness great.

Then calmly she repeated the eighth chapter of Romans: 'For I reckon that the sufferings of this present time are not worthy to be compared with the glory which shall be revealed in us.'

Just moments before the tide would have drowned her for sure some of the soldiers rushed into the water, unbound her, and carried Margaret ashore.

As soon as she had recovered, she was asked if she would pray for the King. She answered, 'I wish the salvation of all men.'

A friend nearby urged her just to say the words 'God save the King.'

'God save him if He will, for it is his salvation I desire,' was the calm reply.

'She has said it, she has said it!' cried the friend to the officer in charge; but it was not enough. When she was asked if she would sign the abjuration oath and declare that the King, not Christ, was the head of the church she exclaimed 'I will not. I am one of Christ's children; let me go.'

And with these brave words on her lips she was once again tied to the stake and this time left until the waves had completely covered her.

LOOK IT UP

1. Worship – what does this word mean? Look it up in a dictionary.

2. Do you think there are places where people worship today instead of going to church to worship God? What people are seen as most important by ordinary men and women today?

3. Deuteronomy 5:8 says that we are not to worship anything or anyone but God. The Bible gives us other instructions about worship what are these? Read the following verses: Psalm 100:2; Romans 12:1; John 4:24.

ELIZABETH GAUNT
She Suffered for Her Mercy

When your country is in the middle of political upheaval and the powers that be are issuing decrees against this, that and the next thing it can be difficult to live your life as a normal citizen. You may have to make a choice between the quiet life and a life of integrity. As a Christian you will have a strong desire to follow God's Word and help his people. But the government or those in charge of your society may not see things exactly as you see them. You could find yourself in trouble for simply doing someone a good turn.

How would you feel if you were betrayed to the authorities by someone you had risked your life to help?

You find yourself having to face the scaffold instead of them! This is what happened to one elderly woman named Elizabeth Gaunt. Because of her good nature and kind disposition she was betrayed and martyred.

Elizabeth Gaunt had a good reputation and she was looked upon kindly by many of her friends and neighbours. If you were ever in need of help Elizabeth was the one to turn to.

She wasn't just a woman who would only help her friends. It didn't matter if you were new to town and hadn't a penny to your name, you could always find a bite to eat and a warm hearth at Elizabeth's.

However, in the England of 1685 it didn't matter if you were a kindly old woman, much loved by your community. If you angered the authorities by your religious views you could face a death sentence.

And this is what happened to Elizabeth Gaunt. Two years earlier a plot had been hatched to assassinate King Charles II as he passed by a placed called Rye House. Nothing happened and the plot was abandoned, but the culprits were still betrayed to the government so the men had to flee for their lives.

One of the plotters, James Burton, pleaded with Elizabeth to hide him in her house. 'I'm being pursued and if caught I'll be hung for sure – possibly burned. I've got a young family who need me. You're my last hope.'

Elizabeth did what she always did – and helped. She definitely went the extra mile. Not only did she assist the man in his escape, but she also gave him all her precious savings.

However, what happened next was totally unexpected.

The government issued a proclamation that any one who gave evidence that lead to the arrest of those who took part in the plot to kill the king would be given immunity from prosecution.

James Burton immediately jumped at the chance to save himself. A deal was struck. James would testify against Elizabeth in court if the authorities agreed to set him free afterwards. Bizarrely, the government agreed to this. So the man who plotted to kill the King was set free and the old woman who had generously helped another was taken up before Judge Jeffreys – a notoriously unjust man.

'My fault,' Elizabeth wrote in the days prior to her death, 'was one which a prince might well have forgiven. I did but relieve a poor family and I must die for it.'

So on 23 October 1685 Elizabeth Gaunt was burned at the stake – the last woman to be burned alive in England for treason.

You could say that she should have been wiser, but she was a tender and generous woman. That really was the extent of her crime and she should not have been killed for it. Some said afterwards that if she had not held firm to many of her beliefs, one of which included pacifism she might have been allowed to live.

LOOK IT UP

1. Betrayal – what does this word mean? Look it up in a dictionary.

2. Can you think of different people in the Bible who were betrayed by people close to them?

3. It can be hard sometimes to know who we should trust, but we can always trust our Heavenly Father – God. Look up the following Bible verses which talk about trusting in God: Psalm 9:10; Psalm 13:5; Psalm 19:7; Psalm 20:7; Psalm 56:3; Psalm 118:8; Proverbs 3:5; John 14:1

MARIE DURAND
Imprisoned for Life

Perhaps it's not much effort for you to imagine that you're fifteen years old – but perhaps this is an age that you haven't reached yet – or that is long gone. However, try for a moment to picture what it was like for a fifteen year old girl in the 1700s. You are living in France and you are just at the beginning of your adult life. You have many things to look forward to. Your parents are planning your betrothal and soon you will be starting a home and family of your own. Perhaps you hope that you will live close to your family and friends. You probably have all sorts of plans for your future, but languishing in prison for thirty-eight years certainly isn't one of them. It would not have been part of Marie Durand's plans either! However, Marie Durand lived at a time in France where a Huguenot wasn't allowed to make plans unless those plans involved submitting to the King.

Marie's family was a well known Protestant or Huguenot family. Often worship meetings were held in the Durand home. They lived in Bouchet-de-Pransles and her brother, Pierre, was a minister. He was in fact being pursued by the authorities – but was successful in avoiding their clutches.

However, as the search continued Marie's father realised that it wasn't just Pierre that was in danger. The whole Durand family could be thrown into prison.

Quickly he arranged for Marie to be married to Matthew Serres.

'This marriage may save you from arrest,' he told his young daughter. 'It is my hope that your husband will be able to protect you.'

In the year 1728, not long after the marriage, Marie's father was arrested. In 1730 Marie and her husband were also put in jail. It was the beginning of what would be a long prison sentence. However, it was one which Marie put to good use.

She was incarcerated in The Tower of Constance which stood on some swampy ground near the Rhone River, in Aigues Mortes not far from the Mediterranean. During the wars between the Protestants and Catholics that followed the Reformation, the tower had fallen into Protestant control. However, in 1632 Louis XIII regained it and it was eventually turned into a women's prison.

The conditions were dreadful. All the female prisoners were kept in an upper room and only a little light and air was allowed in through some very narrow windows. During the winter the tower was freezing cold, but during the summer it was boiling hot. However, when Marie entered the tower she was like a breath of fresh air to the destitute criminals. Even the most hardened recognised Marie as a truly pious young girl. They may not have trusted in her God at first, but they did believe that Marie was different. They respected her for that.

For the next thirty-eight years Marie organised what was needed for the prisoner's physical and spiritual well being. She nursed the sick and wrote letters for the illiterate. She read out loud to those who couldn't read for themselves and encouraged everyone to join in with the hymns that she loved to sing.

Marie was thankfully allowed to send letters out of the prison. Frequently she would send letters to churches and government departments pleading for improved prison conditions. Some of her requests were granted and throughout her time in prison she remained firm in her faith in Christ.

Eventually the prison conditions at The Tower of Constance became so infamous that the governor of Languedoc ordered that the captives should be released. The king objected strongly, but soon Marie and the others were set free.

Christian Heroines

It was a different world that she entered from the one that she had left as a fifteen-year-old girl. She was now fifty-three years old. Her husband, her father and her brother were all dead. For the rest of her life she was supported by other Christians who cared for her until her death in 1776.

LOOK IT UP

1. Pious – what does this word mean? Look it up in a dictionary.

2. What would you feel like if you were put in prison? Would this be a positive or negative experience for you? How did Marie feel do you think? Can you think of other people in the Bible who were put in prison? How did they behave in jail?

3. You don't have to be in prison to be in chains. Freedom is something very precious, but even people who are not in jail can still be slaves. When we do not give our lives and love to God we are in fact slaves to sin and wrong doing. Look up these Bible verses to find out what the Bible says about freedom: Psalm 116:16; Psalm 118:5; Psalm 119:32; John 8:32; John 8:36; Romans 6:22.

MODERN MISSIONARIES AND CHRISTIANS

For the sake of this book we are going to say that the modern era begins when the first American missionary left that nation's shores for the far east. That may seem like history to some of you, but the 1800s saw the beginning of many great missionary endeavours. Modern day missions owe much to the men and women who took the first steps to travel to these unknown lands. Advances in travel and then in engineering, science, and technology were all used to the glory of God through these lives of Christian service. Much of what these men and women did in the 19th century paved the way for the twentieth and twenty first centuries. However, often when we look over the past struggles and trials of the church and its members we forget that the twentieth century was the most violent century that the world has ever seen. There have been more Christian martyrs during the last 100 years than there has ever been in the history of the church.

The violence continues and we shouldn't be surprised. Jesus himself said to his followers:

'If the world hates you, keep in mind that it hated me first. If you belonged to the world, it would love you as its own. As it is, you do not belong to the world, but I have chosen you out of the world. That is why the world hates you. Remember the words I spoke to you: "No servant is greater than his master." If they persecuted me, they will persecute you also. If they obeyed my teaching, they will obey yours also' (John 15:18-20 NIV).

THINGS TO DO:

1. Do some research into missionary organisations. Here are two to start you off with: Overseas Missionary Fellowship (now OMF International); Wycliffe Bible Translators.

2. Take out an atlas and look up the location of any place that is mentioned in the stories.

3. Start a missionary prayer board at church or Sunday School. Keep it up to date with the names and locations of people who are serving God at home and overseas. Encourage others to pray for these people.

ANN HASSELTINE JUDSON
A First Lady

In the modern era of transatlantic travel and gap years, jetting off to the other side of the world is still romantic and adventurous, but it doesn't have the same impact that it once did. If you lived in the early 1800s you would have felt that you lived in a modern age. And of course that was true. Many advances had been made at the turn of that century. However, it was still almost unheard of for young women to cross oceans to other lands. Even if your husband was with you, it was a very daring thing to do. Women weren't allowed to do a lot of things back then and travelling across the globe was almost unheard of for the female sex.

However, Ann Hasseltine Judson did just that.

In 1812 not long after her marriage to Adoniram Judson, she left behind her family and friends to travel to India. She was now seeing a teenage prayer fulfilled for one day as a young Christian she had asked God, 'Direct me in Thy service, and I ask no more. I would not choose my position of work, or place of labour. Only let me know Thy will, and I will readily comply.'

But the Judsons' original plans to work in India were soon thwarted. The government there was against any missionary activity and they were ordered to leave. This meant that Adoniram and Ann had to find somewhere else to work for the Lord and they were directed towards Burma.

This was a land of over fifteen million people who had never heard the good news of the Lord Jesus Christ. There was no one there who had heard that there was a cure for the problem of sin, that there was a God who was loving and merciful. Instead there were thousands upon thousands of men, women and children who were pursuing false gods and false hopes. Ann prayed, 'O thou Light of the world, dissipate the thick darkness which covers Burma, and let thy light arise and shine. O display thy grace and power among the Burmese. Subdue them to thyself and make them thy chosen people.'

With hard work and commitment, the Judsons soon got the hang of the Burmese language and began to work towards translating the Bible. Within three years they had translated the gospel of Matthew.

However, in 1823 war broke out between the United Kingdom and Burma. Even though America was not involved, the Burmese assumed that Americans were on the side of their enemy. Adoniram was thrown into what was called the 'death prison.' Ann, two months pregnant was placed under house arrest. However, after much pleading she finally managed to persuade the authorities to let her bring provisions to her husband in prison.

There she found Adoniram in a poor state of health. When he fell sick with tropical fever, Ann was forced to take on all the duties of care for her husband. With a new born baby to care for, she also had a dangerously sick husband in need of constant attention. Ann also had to look after the translation work that they had already completed. At the time of Adoniram's imprisonment a portion of the precious manuscript was buried for safety. Later on, Ann dug it back up again to protect it from decay. She sewed it into a pillowcase and gave it to her husband to look after. Even though he was sick, it was felt that the manuscript was probably safer under his protection.

However, despite his physical condition the authorities decided to move him secretly to another prison. Ann knew nothing about it until she visited him as usual one day and discovered his absence. She then had to carry her three-month-old daughter for eight long miles over hard and difficult terrain to another prison at Oung-pen-le.

When she arrived there, she was allowed to share a room with the jailor and his family, but Ann soon fell victim to smallpox. She also discovered that the manuscript was missing. When Adoniram had entered the new prison the jailor had searched the prisoner's belongings, seized the hidden manuscript and thrown it out on a rubbish heap.

Thankfully a man, Moung Ing, was a faithful friend and supporter of the Judsons. He discovered the translation and rescued it, returning it once again to the mission house where it was kept in safety.

As time wore on, however, the situation seemed to become ever more desperate. Ann could see no way out. She was certain that Adoniram would die and that she would be forced into slavery. But even in those trying circumstances her trust in her Lord and Saviour Jesus Christ gave her strength. She knew that there was another world beyond this one where Jesus ruled. There was no grief or disease there.

However, despite her doubts in December 1825, Adoniram was eventually released. Joyfully, Ann was reunited with him until she died from a fever on 24 October 1826. She was thirty-seven years old. Her infant daughter also died several months later.

Adoniram remained in Burma to complete the work that he and Ann had begun together. It was twenty-four years before he completed the translation of the entire Bible into Burmese, but by the time of his death in 1850 there were sixty-three churches in the country with many more missionaries working there.

LOOK IT UP

1. Can you find Burma in an atlas or on a globe?

2. Do you wonder what God has in store for you? Do you want to know what his will is for your life? Look up Romans 12:2 to find out what you should do.

3. There are other verses in the Bible that tell us what God's will is for us. Read: 1 Thessalonians 5:18; 1 Peter 2:15; 1 Peter 3:17; 2 Corinthians 8:5. He has also given us specific commandments to follow: Read Exodus chapter 20.

MARIANNA SLOCUM
Hopes and Dreams and Happy Ever After

We all have images of the perfect romance. You've seen it on Hollywood movies and read about them in classic fiction. The guy always gets the girl and the words 'happily ever after' feature somewhere towards the end of the story. Well, Marianna Slocum had a romance, but it wasn't the happily ever after kind.

Marianna had long been convinced that she was to work in missions. She had joined the Summer Institute of Linguistics and was preparing to become a missionary Bible translator. Another young man was on the same track. Bill Bentley had already begun his work in Mexico, but was still attending training sessions with Wycliffe Bible Translators. After his training was completed, he would return to his work amongst the Tzeltal people. Marianna accepted an assignment in the Chol tribe which wasn't that far from where Bill was stationed.

Both the languages of the Chol and Tzeltal peoples were Mayan languages. It hadn't been that long since the Mexican government had been persuaded of the necessity of increasing the literacy of the native population. So Wycliffe Bible Translators had been allowed into the country to set things in motion.

That wasn't all that was set in motion. With Marianna not that far away, Bill often visited her to discuss various language problems or other issues. Then one day he brought Marianna a heart shaped cookie. Their relationship began to change. In February 1941 he asked her to marry him and a wedding was planned for August at Marianna's home in Philadelphia.

It must have been an exciting time for the young couple. Shortly before their wedding they returned to the United States to take part in a missionary convention and do some sightseeing before the wedding.

When the wedding was only six days away they returned to Philadelphia. There were no signs to warn them of what was to come.

The next morning Bill did not come down to breakfast. Marianna's father went upstairs to wake him up only to find him dead. He had died during the night of congenital heart failure.

Marianna had many phone calls to make that day, but one of them was to the head of the mission they belonged to. his name was Cameron Townsend. She had one question to ask him, 'May I go to Bill's tribe and finish the work he began there?' she asked.

Cameron answered yes. He simply couldn't refuse the young woman's request.

The plans that had been made for a wedding had to be put to one side for now there was a funeral to organise. Later, Bill's body was sent back to his family's home near Topeka, Kansas where a headstone was put up above his grave. It read:

William C. Bentley,

1913-1941,

Ambassador for Christ to Mexico.

Bill's work in Mexico was done. Marianna's wasn't.

The work was hard and discouraging at times. This was after all a language that didn't even have a written alphabet. It had never had one, as all their stories and traditions had been passed down verbally through the generations. Often lonely, Marianna worked among the Tzeltals carrying on the work that her beloved fiancé had begun. However, years later in 1947 another woman named Florence joined her in the work there. God used these two women to bring four hundred converts to himself.

In 1956, fifteen years after she had taken over Bill's work the first Tzeltal New Testament was completed.

A big shipment arrived on a small aircraft and soon queues of Indians were lining up to buy their own copy.

Marianna and Florence had completed a mammoth task. Not only were the Tzeltals reading their own Bibles and running their own churches, they were also taking care of their own health needs. The life in that tribe had dramatically changed for the better under the influence of Marianna and Florence. You would have understood it if they had wanted to remain there, carrying on the work and enjoying the fruits of it. However, both women felt the call to move on. And move on they did. First to work among the Bachajon people and finally to a mission in the Columbia mountains.

Losing her fiancé had been hard for Marianna. She could easily have felt that there was no point in going on – but she trusted in the Lord God. The heartbreaking event, the struggles, the tears and the hard work were all for God's glory. She had gone to work with Bill's people, but she had done it for God.

LOOK IT UP

1. Take some time to look at the country of Mexico on a map. Think about the problems and difficulties missionaries must face when they travel to new cultures and have to write down languages never written before.

2. Do you wonder why God let these things happen to Marianna? It is a very tragic thing for a young woman to lose her fiancée just days before their wedding. Look up the following Bible verses. What do these verses teach us about Marianne's situation and about our own? Genesis 50:20; Romans 8:28.

3. There are other verses from God's Word that can give us comfort when we are sad. Read: Psalm 34:17-19; Isaiah 41:10; Matthew 11:28; 2 Corinthians 1:3-4; 1 Peter 5:6-7. God gives us peace and even joy in times of sorrow.

BETTY STAM
Living For Jesus

Have you ever put something on hold – held back until you were sure it was the right thing to do? Perhaps there is something that you really want, yet you're not sure if it is the right thing for you. Perhaps all this talk of holding back and putting off is totally foreign. You may be the sort of person who just goes for it – following your heart and not your head. Well, Betty Stam wanted to follow her heart and her head, but knew that she had to follow God.

She had known this from a very early age. At age ten she wrote a poem which said:

Christian Heroines

'I cannot live like Jesus example though he be
For he was strong and selfless and I am tied to me.
But I have asked my Jesus
To live his life in me...
Behold his warm, his tangible
His dear humanity.'

And then aged eighteen she wrote another poem,

'Lord, I give up all my own plans and purposes
All my own desires and hopes
And accept Thy will for my life.
I give myself, my life, my all
Utterly to Thee to be Thine forever.'

But then she met this really great guy at a prayer meeting! His name was John and he liked her too, however, Betty and this guy John had both committed their lives to missionary service. They were going to share the good news of Jesus Christ with others and that was going to be the main focus of their lives. They weren't doing this because they thought it would make them better Christians or because they had any ambition to travel or work abroad – it was simply because God had called them to this work and they wanted to glorify him.

John and Betty both felt called to China despite the escalating violence against Christians in that country.

They both discussed their attraction to each other as well as their call to mission and decided that marriage might hinder their work for God. So Betty left for China in 1931 without John.

John followed a year later and when he and Betty eventually met up again in Shanghai, they agreed to an engagement and were finally married.

The first year of married life was spent in Suancheng learning the language. But just because they didn't know the language didn't mean that they couldn't share the gospel. They always had Chinese Christian literature to hand out. Before too long they began to get a better grasp of the language and they were able to teach and preach to the native Chinese.

In 1934 John and Betty Stam gave birth to a little girl whom they named Helen Priscilla. In the same year they moved to the province of Anhwei.

'Weren't missionaries evacuated from that station not so long ago?' someone asked.

But John and Betty assured them that they had been told there was no danger now. However, as it turned out the Stams had been totally misinformed about the area they were moving to.

Just a few weeks after their initial arrival, Communist soldiers were beating down their door. The little family of three was held captive, but thankfully John was allowed to send a letter to their mission headquarters.

The letter ended with the heartfelt words, 'May God be glorified whether by life or by death.'

The day after their capture the couple and the infant baby were marched to Tsingteh where their captors paraded them in front of the towns folk. A passer-by asked John where they were going. He replied, 'We don't know where they are going, but we are going to heaven.'

One Chinese Christian named Zhang Shuisheng pleaded for their lives, but with a quick swing of the sword John was decapitated. Betty, trembling, did not cry out. Instead she knelt down beside the body of her husband in prayer. As she knelt the same sword that had killed her husband took her life also. It was a terrible death, but a glorious welcome awaited them in their real home – heaven.

However, the message of the gospel was still preached – despite the persecution by the Communists. One Chinese pastor stood up and proclaimed, 'You have seen these wounded bodies, and you pity your friends for their suffering and death. But you should know that they are children of God and are at this moment in the presence of their heavenly Father. They came to China to tell you about the great love of God, that you might believe in the Lord Jesus Christ and be eternally saved. You have heard their message. Remember, it is true. Their death proves it. Do not forget what they told you – repent, and believe the gospel.'

The same evangelist did his utmost to find baby Helen – but no one was sure if she was alive or dead. There was no sign of her anywhere until an old woman came up and whispered to him, 'The foreign baby is still alive.' The evangelist found Helen wrapped in a blanket quite oblivious to what had taken place in the last twenty-four hours. But what were the Chinese Christians to do with her? As it turned out in the moments before her execution, Betty had packed essential provisions for her little girl. Ten dollars had been hidden inside some diapers. So thanks to her mother's forward thinking and the courage of the Chinese believers, Helen was smuggled to safety and raised in the home of her grandparents.

In China there is a grave stone which commemorates the lives of her parents, two missionary martyrs:

John Cornelius Stam

18 January, 1907

'That Christ may be magnified whether by life or by death.' Philippians 1:20

Elizabeth Scott Stam

His Wife

22 February 1906

'For me to live is Christ and to die is gain.'

Philippians 1:21

The grave also bears the name of the Chinese Christian who pleaded for their safe release. Despite John's final plea for mercy before he was beheaded, this brave man also met his death alongside them.

LOOK IT UP

1. Look at the land of China on the map. Take some time to think about the many millions of Christians who live there today. It is said that there are now more Christians living in China than there are people living in the United Kingdom.

2. John Stam's verse on the grave stone says that Christ should be magnified. What does magnified mean? How can we magnify Christ? Look up the following words spoken by John the Baptist in John 3:30.

3. Betty's verse on the grave says that to live is Christ, but to die is gain. How can a Christian say that? What is it about life after death which is so desirable? Read these Bible verses: Matthew 5:12; Matthew 6:20; Hebrews 11:16; Revelation 7:16-17; Ephesians 5:5.

CORRIE TEN BOOM
Knowing How to Love

I am sure that all of us have somebody in our past that we would like to meet up with again, perhaps an old school friend or neighbour. On the other hand, perhaps there is someone who you would travel miles to avoid, the memory of what they did to you and how they made you feel is too sharp and painful.

Knowing how to love and how to forgive can be difficult. Bitterness is a poison. This is something that Corrie ten Boom had to learn at various times during her life.

She is well known today for her heroic actions which were influential in saving the lives of eight hundred Jews, but as a young woman Corrie ten Boom had hopes and dreams as any young woman did. She was part of a committed Christian family. Her father, Casper, was the stalwart head of the household and a loving and constant presence in her life.

The family owned a watch shop in Haarlem, Holland where they lived in some rooms situated above the shop.

Corrie never married, but she had had hopes of marriage once which never materialized. The young man whom she believed was God's choice for her left the area for a time, only to return with his new wife. This was a deep shock for Corrie at first, but her family sympathetically helped her through it. Bringing her heartache to God, she asked him to help her love this young man in a different way, in a way that honoured God. She knew that left to herself she could so easily give way to a bitterness of spirit.

Without a husband and family of her own to love, Corrie poured her heart and her life into God's service. In 1920 Corrie began to train as a watchmaker like her father and in 1922 became Holland's first licensed female watchmaker. In 1923 she helped organise girls' clubs which eventually grew to be very popular.

However, all this was to change when the Nazis invaded the Netherlands in 1940. Corrie's club was banned and only clubs organised by the Nazis were permitted. It wasn't long though before Corrie and her family became active in the Dutch resistance. Their chief duty was to hide refugees. Corrie, Betsie, her sister, and their father were committed to helping God's chosen people the Jews. Many Jews escaped certain death with their help. How did they do this? Well they created a secret room at the back of Corrie's bedroom – a small compact space where several people could hide just in case the Nazis decided to search the ten Boom's apartment.

An alarm system was set up so that whenever an unexpected visitor arrived, the residents of the house could be alerted to the fact. The Jewish residents would then immediately remove all trace of their existence and disappear into the secret room which was a hidden annexe at the back of Corrie's bedroom.

Corrie had to make use of a whole network of contacts in order to keep the hiding place in operation. There were ration cards and other documentation to sort out for the illegal residents in 'The Hiding Place'. One day the ten Booms were betrayed to the Nazis and the whole family was arrested and put in jail.

They were all sent to Scheveningen prison. Moments before the family was separated Casper ten Boom managed to gather them altogether as he recited some verses from Psalm 91.

He that dwelleth in the secret place of the Most High shall abide under the shadow of the Almighty.

I will say of the Lord, He is my refuge and my fortress: my God; in him will I trust.

Surely he shall deliver thee from the snare of the fowler,

and from the noisome pestilence.

He shall cover thee with his feathers, and under his wings shalt thou trust:

his truth shall be thy shield and buckler.

These verses would be a comfort and strength to them over the time of persecution that lay ahead.

While in prison, a package was allowed to be delivered to Corrie. She happened to notice the strange way in which the address was slanted on the front of the parcel. 'It is almost as though they are wanting me to look at the stamp. Perhaps they are?' Corrie thought.

Gingerly she peeled away the stamp from the parcel and discovered a secret message written underneath. 'All of the watches are safe.' It was a secret code to tell Corrie that all of the Jews in the secret room had escaped.

However, it wasn't all good news that Corrie heard. Her father died ten days after his capture and Corrie was to be sent to the Vught political concentration camp. Both Corrie and Betsie were eventually sent to the notorious Ravensbruck concentration camp in Germany in September 1944.

While they were there, the two sisters set up a Bible study in the camp in order to help their fellow inmates find comfort and hope through God's Word.

The conditions in the camp were truly dreadful. The food was poor and there was very little of it and the shelter was cold, cramped and filthy. Many people died in these camps through malnutrition and disease. However, Betsie ten Boom was an example of great Christian endurance and love during that time. She taught Corrie how to be thankful in all circumstances. This was something that Corrie couldn't understand at first. How could she be thankful for the dreadful conditions that the Nazis kept them in?

'Look at these fleas!' Corrie exclaimed one day. 'How can we be thankful for fleas?'

Betsie thought about this and pointed out to her sister that because their hut was so full of fleas and lice, the Nazi guards gave it a wide berth and pretty much left the woman in their hut to their own devices. 'Because of these fleas we are left alone to have our Bible studies in peace!' Betsie smiled. So Corrie had to admit that, yes, she could thank God for the fleas.

The two sisters were unwavering in their belief in God and his love, even during what must have been one of the darkest times of their life. Corrie and Betsie would even share the news of God's love with the Gestapo who interrogated them. These men were the intelligence arm of the Nazi machine and would torture the prisoners in order to get information out of them. However, Betsie and Corrie would always take advantage of these interrogations and use them to share the good news of Jesus Christ.

It was Betsie, however, who was often the source of spiritual wisdom and comfort for her younger sister. In the weeks before Betsie died she encouraged Corrie with the following words, 'There is no pit so deep that God's love is not deeper still.' She also persuaded Corrie to forgive the Dutchman who had betrayed their family to the Nazis. This was something very hard for Corrie to do. Betsie suggested that she prayed for the man.

'Pray for that devil,' Corrie raged. 'Never!'

'Think how he hates himself,' Betsie pointed out. 'Think how he too suffers.'

So Corrie found herself forced to pray for the man and to her surprise she found that this act of prayer changed her. For the first time since she had learned of the man's identity, she slept without bitterness and anger.

Two days after Betsie's death Corrie was released from Ravensbruck as the result of a clerical error. As it turned out all the female prisoners in Corrie's unit were put to death the following week so Corrie could testify to the fact that, 'God does not have problems. Only plans.'

And one of God's plans for after the war was for Corrie to set up rehabilitation centres for those who had suffered in the concentration camps. It had been something she and Betsie had planned together as they waited longingly for freedom.

'Corrie,' Betsie had said, 'after the war, we must tell people how good God is. No one will be able to say that they have suffered worse than us. We can tell them how wonderful God is and how his love will fill our lives. If only we will give up our hatred and bitterness.'

Betsie had dreamed of a house where they would live once all the horror was over. It would be a place where they would help others like themselves to recover from the ordeal of the concentration camps. Corrie was sceptical at first, but Betsie persisted, 'I believe God is going to give us that house.'

Though Betsie didn't see it – a house was given to them from a woman whose son had safely returned from one of the camps. When Corrie saw the house she smiled. It was exactly as Betsie had imagined it would be!

However, there was one further lesson for Corrie to learn. It was a lesson of forgiveness.

Corrie found herself one Lord's Day standing in the church aisle looking into the face of one of her ex-prison guards. He was humbly offering her his hand. Yet Corrie didn't know if she had it in her to forgive him. Anxiously she prayed to God for help, which he gave.

'For a long moment we grasped each other's hands, the former guard and the former prisoner. I had never known God's love so intensely as I did then.'

Corrie's later life was active and busy as she became a Christian speaker and writer. In the 1950s, for example, she spoke in sixty-four different countries as far apart as Argentina and Vietnam. In 1949, however, another part of Corrie's life came full circle when she was able to raise the money to rent the out of use concentration camp of Darmstadt in Germany. Corrie was able to make it into a refuge for displaced persons and ex-prisoners. What had once been a place of evil and torture was now a place of love and rebuilding.

After suffering a stroke and losing the power of speech, Corrie's life ended in 1983 in the country she had adopted as her own – the United States of America. Her books are still published and widely read across the world. An award winning film was even made about her life and they called it, *The Hiding Place*.

LOOK IT UP

1. What is the dictionary definition of forgiveness? Do you see forgiveness as an example of someone being weak or strong?

2. The Bible tells us that we need forgiveness – why? What have we done against God that needs forgiveness? 1 John 1:9.

3. When God forgives our sins he does something more than simply forgive? Look up Hebrews 8:12 to find out what.

4. Who is the only one through whom we can receive forgiveness of sins? Acts 13:38

JUST LIKE YOU AND ME!

Imagine that it is you who is standing face to face with a policeman and that he has an order for your arrest. You are in your front porch and the squad car is parked on the street outside. Your neighbours are looking on, but as you are taken away from your home and family nobody does anything to help you. You are being taken to prison and the only thing you are guilty of is being a Christian. For many people in our world today persecution of this kind and worse is a stark reality. But perhaps you live in a country where the very idea that this could happen to you seems ridiculous. If this is what you are thinking, keep in mind that countries and governments can change in the blink of an eye. Your world might end up being a very different place one day. Physical persecution may be illegal in your country, but as many Christians across the world can testify, freedoms that took generations to build up can disappear overnight.

At the moment you may not be in danger of a jail sentence, but at the very least you may be ridiculed for believing in Jesus. If your faith is something that goes beyond church and impacts every day of your life, then it is likely that at some point you will be exposed to cruel jokes. Just remember that Jesus Christ was mocked by the Roman Centurions. His response was one of grace as he prayed to his Father to forgive his enemies.

Christians can find themselves passed over for promotion because they aren't willing to compromise their faith in Christ. When a Christian wants to keep the Lord's Day special they can end up in conflict with employers who do not understand their views. This can have implications for family finances. It can effect a Christian's choices about where they can afford to live, and what schools they send their children to.

If you live in a country where it is illegal to physically persecute people for their faith that is something to be thankful for. Make the most of it. Other Christians from other countries do not have the privileges that you have. If you have a Bible in your own language you are very blessed – so take the opportunity to read it. You do not know if you will always be allowed such freedom.

If you are one of those Christians who has experienced physical persecution then remember that Jesus Christ also suffered. He understands the troubles that you face. Not only did he undergo the mocking sneers of his enemies, but he was also whipped severely and nailed to a cross. He was willing to die in order to save his people from their sins.

For all of us who face troubles because of our faith in Christ, there is a special message in the book of Revelation.

'Do not be afraid of what you are about to suffer.
I tell you, the devil will put some of you in prison
to test you, and you will suffer persecution...
Be faithful, even to the point of death,
and I will give you the crown of life.'
Revelation 2:10 (NIV)

INSPIRING STORIES OF MARTYRS BY
IRENE HOWAT

ISBN: 978-1-84550-036-8

Ten girls grew up to become women who didn't
give in. They chose to do the right thing instead of
the easy thing. Blandina; Perpetua; Lady Jane Grey;
Anne Askew; Lysken Dirks; Marion Harvey; Margaret
Wilson; Judith Weinberg; Betty Stam; Esther John. In
a world where we give in too easily – be inspired by
those who didn't!

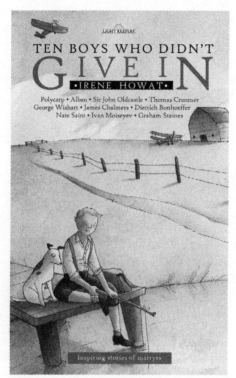

INSPIRING STORIES OF MARTYRS BY
IRENE HOWAT
ISBN: 978-1-84550-035-1

Ten boys grew up to become men who didn't give in. They chose to do the right thing instead of the easy thing. Polycarp; Alban; John Oldcastle; Thomas Cranmer; George Wishart; James Chalmers; Dietrich Bonhoeffer; Nate Saint; Ivan Moiseyev; Graham Staines. In a world where we give in too easily – be inspired by those who didn't!

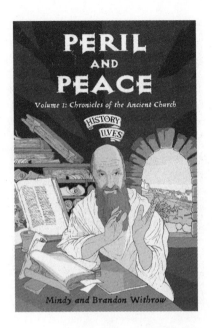

PERIL AND PEACE BY
MINDY & BRANDON WITHROW
ISBN: 978-1-84550-082-5

Read the stories of Paul, Polycarp, Justin, Origen,
Cyprian, Constantine, Athanasius, Ambrose,
Augustine, John Chrysostom, Jerome, Patrick, and
Benedict. People from the early and ancient church
and discover the roots of Christianity. From the
apostle Paul to Benedict you can discover how those
in the early church still influence church today. You
will see the young and developing church struggling
and growing in a hostile and difficult world.

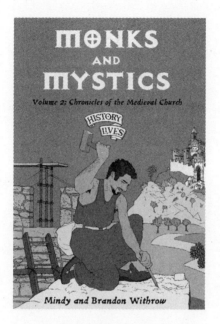

MONKS AND MYSTICS BY
MINDY & BRANDON WITHROW
ISBN: 978-1-84550-083-2

Read the stories of Gregory the Great, Boniface,
Charlemagne, Constantine Methodius, Vladimir, Anselm
of Canterbury, Bernard of Clairvaux, Francis of Assisi,
Thomas Aquinas, Catherine of Sienna, John Wyclif and
John Hus. From people of the Medieval church you
can discover how the young Christian church moved
on into another era of time. As the church moves on
through the centuries you can see its people struggling
against persecution and problems from inside and out.

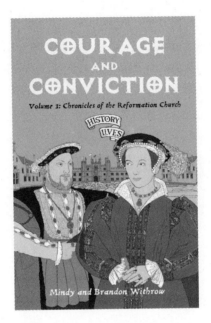

COURAGE AND CONVICTION BY
MINDY & BRANDON WITHROW
ISBN: 978-1-84550-222-5

Read the stories of the reformers in the 16th and 17th centuries who changed the face of the Christian church forever. Meet the German monk, the French scholar, and the Scottish tutor who protested corruption in the church. From Erasmus and Luther to Katherine Parr and William Bradford, God used different personalities in different places to bring sweeping changes to church government and the way we worship. Learn from their mistakes and be encouraged by their amazing strengths and gifts.

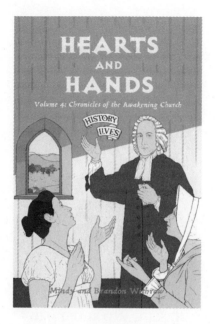

HEARTS AND HANDS BY
MINDY & BRANDON WITHROW
ISBN: 978-1-84550-288-1

Let history come to life, just the way it should do! Read
the stories of the gifted preachers and justice fighters
who led the 1st & 2nd Great Awakenings in the 18th and
19th centuries. Meet the American preacher who started
a national revival in his tiny church. Spend time with the
wealthy English politician and the former American slave
woman who helped abolish slavery in their countries.
Get to know the missionaries who built lasting Christian
communities in China, India, and Africa.

RESCUE AND REDEEM BY
MINDY & BRANDON WITHROW
ISBN: 978-1-84550-433-5

As the modern world exploded with rapid changes,
people around the globe faced overwhelming new
challenges. As Christians arrived for the first time in
other countries, they realized that being a Christian
was about living out the gospel in every culture
and that injustice was everywhere! So they met the
challenges with new ways of communicating Christ's
ancient gospel. From Niijima Jo and Pandita Ramabai
to Dietrich Bonhoeffer and Janani Luwum, they set
out to rescue God's global people and redeem them to
new life in Christ.

Margaret, Agnes and Thomas are not afraid to stand up for what they believe in, but it means that they are forced to leave their home and their parents for a life of hiding on the hills. If you were a covenanter in the 1600's you were the enemy of the King and the authorities. But all you really wanted to do was worship God in the way he told you to in the Bible.

ISBN: 978-1-85792-784-9

The story of Corrie ten Boom has inspired millions of people all over the world. The Watchmaker's Daughter traces the life of this outstanding Christian woman from her childhood in Haarlem, through her suffering in Nazi concentration camps, to her world-wide ministry to the handicapped and underprivileged.

ISBN: 978-1-85792-116-8

CHRISTIAN FOCUS PUBLICATIONS

Christian Focus | Christian Heritage | CF4K | Mentor

Christian Focus Publications publishes books for adults and children under its four main imprints: Christian Focus, CF4K, Mentor and Christian Heritage. Our books reflect our conviction that God's Word is reliable and Jesus is the way to know him, and live for ever with him.

Our children's publication list includes a Sunday School curriculum that covers pre-school to early teens, and puzzle and activity books. We also publish personal and family devotional titles, biographies and inspirational stories that children will love.

If you are looking for quality Bible teaching for children then we have an excellent range of Bible stories and age-specific theological books.

From pre-school board books to teenage apologetics, we have it covered!

Find us at our web page:
www.christianfocus.com

CF4 •K
Because you're never
too young to know Jesus